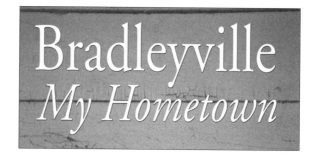

A Collection of Short Stories and Memoirs

By

James Leon Combs

With Contributions from

Jim and Sim Evans

Beaver Creek Publishing, L. L. C.
P.O. Box 2000
Bradleyville, Missouri 65614
888-225-9400
JLCombs13@aol.com
www.bradleyvillehometown.com

Library of Congress Control Number: 2003109540

ISBN: 0-9674853-2-0

Printed and bound in the United States of America
By Jostens Publishing, Topeka, Kansas

Page Composition: Jeff Jasper

Proofreading: Linda Odum

Cover Design: Jeanene Sutton

Website Design: Schilling/Sellmeyer Agency

Cover Photo: Author's great-grandparents, L-R: James Monroe Clark, Mary Elizabeth Rice Clark, Rebecca Jane Clark McPherson, Dr. Elijah T. McPherson (standing in doorway), Anna Clark Morris, Martha Ida Clark Combs (author's grandmother) holding baby Sylvia, John Riley Combs (author's grandfather) with daughters Rosa on his right and Clara on his left, Irvin Sizemore and wife Judy Clark Sizemore, Norman Sizemore and Shade Rick Combs.

CONTENTS

Preface 5

1 • Train Ride to Missouri 6

2 • My Sister and the Cat 12

3 • My First Hero 16

4 • Duke, the Western Horse 20

5 • Hot Acorns and Twenty-two Shells 24

6 • My Cousin Bobby Ray 28

7 • The Booger Man 32

8 • The Gallopin' Goose 35

9 • The Wrestlers 40

10 • Ol' Brownie 44

11 • Brown Lawson 48

12 • My Brother's Keeper 52

13 • Bozie's New Truck 56

14 • Ticket to Daylight 62

15 • My Dad and My Father 81

16 • Welcome to Missouri 85

17 • The Cockfighter 90

18 • My Neighbor, Birdle 97

19 • The Ozark Mountains 107

20 • The Last Public Hanging in America 114

21 • Dad Discovers Electricity.....................118

22 • Coffee Cans Are the Key To Survival 121

23 • Why I'm Afraid of Snakes 123

24 • The Snitch Hunt 125

25 • Old Fox Hunters Like Strong Coffee 132

26 • Bradleyville Today 135

DEDICATION

For my mom, Susie Combs, and Etcyl Combs, my late dad –
they made it possible for me to enjoy the ideal boyhood.

PREFACE

I grew up in a tiny village deep in the Ozarks but never felt deprived of anything. My boyhood on Beaver Creek resembled the lives of Tom Sawyer and Huck Finn on the Mississippi River. We didn't have Thomas Hart Benton, but Leslie Cunningham drew the best pictures I had ever seen. Missourian Harry Truman made a big name for himself, but we didn't consider him a bit better than Ruse Dixon, president of our school board, responsible for constructing our first high school gym.

We read about Jesse and Frank James from St. Joe, but I would bet my bottom dollar Bradleyville's Johnny and Forest Lynch could whip their tails in a no-holds-barred fight. General Black Jack Pershing, leader of American troops in World War I, came from Missouri, but my cousin Roy Combs earned medals for bravery in World War II Pacific battles before a sniper shot and killed him; he was my military hero.

St. Louis and Kansas City were big cities with trains and busy airports, but nothing could be more exciting than watching Brother Floyd Hitchcock from Springfield land his Piper Cub in a nearby pasture to preach to a local crowd gathered there.

Many people in Bradleyville are related, but even if they aren't, they'll still tell your mom and dad if you do something wrong. Everybody hangs together, not always the best thing if you're trying to get away with something.

I grew up in Bradleyville. I loved it when I was young, hated it as a teenager, and love it again now that I'm old.

Bradleyville is my hometown.

James Leon Combs
Summer 2003

1

TRAIN RIDE TO MISSOURI

The day before Christmas, 1936, in Colorado Springs, fifteen-year-old Lourene offered to take care of the baby while her mother Virgie and Aunt Ellen went shopping to get more material for wreaths, an effort to earn a few dollars for Christmas presents. Virgie's hands were cut and bloodied from the sharp wires required for fashioning the wreaths. Lourene had to help her mother dress and even pulled on her hose.

The small fifteen-dollar-a-month rented house sat on a quiet street in a working class neighborhood. A wood-burning stove heated the tiny living room; a cast iron cook stove occupied a large portion of the space in the little kitchen. Rough spots in the wooden floors showed through the worn linoleum covering all four rooms, including two little bedrooms.

Dec. 26, 1936, is a sad day in Colorado Springs as the children of Joe and Virgie Slone return from their parents' funeral. From left are Verna, Lourene, James Leon and Ernie.

Lourene's mother, Virgie Slone, and her Aunt Ellen put on their coats, preparing to go out into the cold winter day. Her mother's imitation fur coat was old and ragged; frayed strings hung from the sleeves.

"Feed the baby," Virgie instructed Lourene. "Then it'll be time for his nap. They's some molasses and biscuits in the kitchen. Ain't no milk now, but he likes molasses and biscuit." When Aunt Ellen opened the door, Lourene felt the cold wind.

The baby, three months short of his second birthday, loved his big "Tister" as he called her, and followed her everywhere, especially when he knew she was fixing something to eat. Lourene lifted him into a rickety homemade high chair and looked into the icebox for butter. No real butter, only an almost-empty jar of peanut butter, so she scraped the sides and bottom with a spoon until she got enough to cover the baby's biscuit. She knew he would really like biscuit and peanut butter covered with black molasses.

Lourene sang "Jingle Bells" happily on that Christmas Eve while the baby laughed and banged a spoon on the wooden highchair tray. He didn't know what Christmas was but knew when his "Tister" was happy. He loved her lyrical voice. Her long brown hair hung in natural curls over her shoulders. High cheekbones, perfect teeth, and a constant smile gave her the look of a movie starlet playing the role of a poor girl. A faded gingham dress and a gray woolen sweater with holes in the elbows covered her slender body.

"Nap time," she announced after the baby ate the biscuit. He didn't resist as she led him to the bedroom, picked up a quilt, blanket and pillow, then came back near the stove. She made a pallet on the floor and lay beside her baby brother. She sang "Silent Night" quietly, enjoying the stove's warmth and the mood of the season. The baby was asleep in minutes. Lourene continued to lie next to him, listening to his regular breathing.

Despite her happy Christmas songs, Lourene was thinking about her family's plight. "How did we end up like this?" she wondered. Only a few months earlier, back in Missouri, they had lived a comfortable life in a big house, owned a new car and had plenty to eat. Her father owned a successful business and was widely respected in the community. Then something happened, something Lourene did not quite understand – the Great Depression. The financial crash led to booze, loss of business, then mental depression. More booze, family squabbles, bankruptcy and separations followed. Her dad finally left home and joined his parents in Colorado. Soon afterward, a letter arrived urging his wife to bring the kids and come out. His father, he said, would help them find a place to live and help him land a job.

Like the Joads in Steinback's *The Grapes of Wrath*, they piled into an old car, driven by Lourene's seventeen-year-old brother Ernie, loaded down with most of their worldly possessions, and headed west. The going was slow, especially at first. Roads in Taney County, where their home was located, were dirt and mud and gravel; sometimes farmers used their tractors to pull cars that were stuck in mud. The Slones made it to Colorado and found the little house.

Lourene's father, Joe, once an outgoing, happy family man and business owner, seemed different when his wife and children arrived in Colorado Springs. Very different: quiet, reserved, sometimes angry. He talked of leaving again, of going to Michigan, where Henry Ford paid big wages to build cars. Every day he drank, got drunk, and promised he was going to stop. He spent more time with his elderly parents, Henry and Martha, than at home with his wife and children.

Lourene's reverie ended, and she heard him walking across the front porch. As she watched her father come through the front door into the little family room, she wanted to cry. The man who once wore a suit and tie and took pride in himself now wore a week's beard and was covered with blood. Ragged clothes hung from his emaciated frame, and an old wool pullover cap covered his head. The splotches of blood came from an afternoon job of plucking feathers from turkeys in a slaughtering plant, the only work he could find in the dark days of the Depression. In the mornings, he stood on downtown streets, trying to sell wreaths Lourene's mother made. Lourene watched as he pulled off an old coat and threw it in the corner, along with the unsold wreaths. She stood by the stove as he walked over, hugged her and gave her a rare kiss on the cheek. He smelled of cheap wine, the odor of constant drinking. He shuffled into one of the little bedrooms and fell face down on the bed. Lourene started to go in but thought she heard him sobbing and stopped. She closed the door instead.

An hour later her mother came through the front door carrying two small paper bags. One contained wreath materials, the other a Christmas present for the baby. Virgie walked quietly across the living room and motioned Lourene to follow her into the kitchen, where she placed the bags on the table. The baby continued napping as his mother sat at the kitchen table, proudly holding a red and white snowsuit, beaming as she showed it to her teenage daughter.

Joe Slone opened the bedroom door and stepped into the room. He walked over to Lourene's mother and tried to kiss her, but she jokingly pushed him away, saying, "Joe, stop it." The loud bang shocked Lourene. She had not seen the gun. She saw her mother's head lurch forward, spurting blood onto the table, then watched as her body fell to the floor. She lay on her back, eyes wide open, staring at nothing, a pool of blood forming around her head. Terror gripped the girl. Her father stood motionless, gun in hand, staring down at his dying wife. He looked surprised. Lourene screamed and stared as the baby ran crying to his mother, falling upon her, clutching her bloody clothes, unable to understand the blank stare. Joe Slone placed the gun to his own head and fired, crumpling onto Virgie's lifeless body, almost falling on the baby. His body twitched and blood spurted from his head. Terrified, Lourene ran from the kitchen, through the living room and out the front door.

Across the street at the home of neighbor Anne Lowe, Lourene screamed hysterically, "My father shot my mother all to pieces! My father killed my mother! Oh, my God, he shot and killed my mother and my baby brother!"

Anne Lowe ran into her front yard to look at the little house across the narrow street. Other neighbors stepped out of their houses. Anne saw the baby standing at the latched screen door, pushing, screaming. She thought a madman was inside, but someone had to get the baby. Without hesitating, Anne ran across the street, through the front gate and onto the porch. She jerked the door open, grabbed the baby, and raced back across the street to her house. Blood covered the baby's face and hands.

Police cars and ambulances arrived in minutes. Virgie Slone was dead at the scene. Joe Slone died later that night in a Colorado Springs hospital.

Lourene, her brother Ernie, who was working on a nearby ranch when the tragedy struck, and the baby spent the night with their father's sister, Aunt Ellen. The baby cried for his mother and his tricycle. Lourene phoned the tragic news to Verna, her married sister living in California with her husband and year-old son. Verna took the first train from Sacramento and arrived at Colorado Springs on Christmas Day.

Twin hearses wound slowly through the rainy streets the next day to a cemetery not far from the foothills of Pike's Peak. The Slone children, ranging from the twenty-one-month-old baby to twenty-year-old Verna, stood together, still in shock, under an umbrella as the preacher read from the Bible.

Verna left later that day with the baby and Lourene for her home in California, while Ernie went back to his job on the ranch. George Warren, Verna's husband, had just been hired by a Safeway store in Fairfield, California. They hoped he could earn enough to feed the expanding family. Verna was six months pregnant, and George's mother, Ethel Warren, lived with them as well. Two more mouths to feed were not a welcome addition to their already struggling household. Verna helped Lourene find a family in Sacramento where she lived in the attic without cost in exchange for cooking and housecleaning. She later managed to work her way through high school.

George and Verna's little house in Fairfield was crowded. George worked long hours at Safeway for meager wages and came home to a pregnant wife, a year-old son, the orphaned baby and his elderly mother. Trying to cope with financial problems proved too much for him, and his temper often flared. Believing her son had enough problems of his own, Ethel did not approve of her daughter-in-law's decision to bring the baby into their home.

Verna initially intended to raise the baby and her son, Cleo, as twins – they were only a few months apart – but saw it was not going to work and talked with George about what to do. She sent an airmail letter to her mother's brother, Etcyl Combs, and his wife, Susie, in Missouri, telling them she could no longer take care of the baby and asking if they would be able to take him. She received an answer ten days later. Susie wrote, "Etcyl and I would love to adopt the baby. Please send him to us."

The Sacramento heat bore down with a vengeance as Ethel led the little boy to board the train. Lourene cried as she stood by George and Verna, watching the train pull out. Ethel Warren waved from the window, holding up Lourene and Verna's little brother for one last look. The old lady was anxious to deliver the boy and get back home, glad Verna had finally listened to her advice to get rid of the baby. Her patience wore thin on the long train ride to Springfield, Missouri, but she knew the baby problem was about to be solved. They changed trains at Springfield for the final ride to Chadwick, the end of the line.

A smiling Aude Deckard, the mailman between Chadwick and Bradleyville, greeted Ethel and the baby at the train station, ready to deliver the baby to Bradleyville at Etcyl Combs' request. His 1931 Model A Ford stood waiting. August heat and humidity stifled activity, and Aude's old car sometimes heated up. He carried a five-gallon can of water, adding to the car's radiator every few miles. From Garrison to Bradleyville, the Model A Ford followed an old logging truck that stirred up huge clouds of dust from the gravel road, covering the car occupants, who had to keep the windows open to prevent suffocation.

A large smiling young man and his young, attractive wife stood in front of the Bradleyville post office as Aude pulled up. Etcyl Combs opened the door and helped Ethel Warren out. He took the boy, who had slept through most of the dusty ride from Chadwick. Etcyl carried the baby as he and Susie walked toward their old Model A Ford. They drove to their house at the edge of the village, an old structure rented from Joe Selvidge. Susie killed a young rooster that afternoon and prepared a large supper of fried chicken with green beans and mashed potatoes from her garden. The old house was spotless with handmade curtains and doilies decorating used furniture. Susie put the baby in an old secondhand highchair, and scooted him up to the table. Ethel Warren placed her chair beside the baby and put food on his plate. Etcyl and Susie watched their new son's every move, but he didn't want to eat. Ethel offered a drumstick, but he resisted and cried when she tried to force the issue. Etcyl pushed his chair back from the table and removed the boy's plate of food. "My boy, Leon, don't have to eat now if he don't want to," he said. He freed the boy from the highchair and carried his new son to the front porch.

The Great Depression was a dark and tragic time for many families. My relatives, and others in the Ozarks, however, enabled me to live a happy childhood in a rich environment. The death of my biological parents did not shadow my childhood, because I did not learn of it for many years, and my adoptive parents, who were closely related, were very loving and supportive.

As is obvious from other stories in this book, my new parents became my real mom and dad. Never could a boy have a more loving mother than Susie Combs, who worked long days side-by-side with her husband, my dad, Etcyl Combs, yet always managed to cover our kitchen table with delicious and nutritious food. She washed and ironed my clothes and even made many of them on her Singer sewing machine. She was then, and is now at age ninety-two, the greatest mother any child could ever have.

When I was in the first grade, my teacher often read to us at the end of the day as a reward for good behavior. Mrs. Walker read Harold Bell Wright's, The Shepherd of the Hills. *She stopped in her reading to describe the handsome young hero, Young Matt. She said, "Young Matt was a big strong man, very handsome, like Etcyl Combs." Of course, I sat upright in my chair and smiled proudly. No father could have shown more love for his son than Etcyl Combs did for me. He was the perfect dad.*

Despite the morbid beginning of my life, I was blessed with an Ozarks family, not wealthy, but rich in love, faith and plain old goodness.

Several years after my arrival in Missouri, I (left) stand with Dad, Mom, sister Peggy and brother Jerry.

2

My Sister and the Cat

Living at the fork in the gravel road made our little farmhouse an easy target for stray animals. People were always dropping off unwanted cats and dogs. One day we saw a big yellow tomcat prowling around the smokehouse, a small wooden shed where Dad kept smoked hams and sacks of feed for hogs and chickens. He wanted to shoot the cat, but Mom stopped him, arguing that it might be a good "mouser" capable of killing the mice and rats that inevitably invaded the smokehouse. Mom started feeding the cat, just enough to make him welcome, but not enough to keep him from going after rats and mice.

I was ten, my sister, Peggy, seven. After Mom and Dad referred to the cat as "the old tom cat," we called him "Tom." It didn't take long for him to

My little sister Peggy and I play in the front yard of our farmhouse.

start acting as if he owned the place and was doing the family a favor by hanging around. Sometimes he disappeared for two or three days, causing Peggy and me to worry. Dad said he was just "tomcattin' around," whatever that meant. He always came home, often covered with scratch marks from fights with other cats.

Our winter woodpile for the cooking and heating stoves stood a few feet up the hill from the tiny smokehouse. In September, Dad started hauling leftover strips of throwaway wood from the local sawmill that made staves for whiskey barrels. The year Tom showed up, our pile of wood stood at least ten feet high and twenty feet across, made of three-foot-long strips thrown helter-skelter, a perfect hiding place for rabbits, other varmints – and Tom.

One morning we were eating a breakfast of bacon, eggs and gravy spread over freshly baked biscuits, when out of the blue, Mom said to Dad, "How long's it been since you've seen Tom?"

"I don't know," he answered, "maybe a week. He's just tomcattin' around."

She caught Dad right in the middle of sipping his coffee from the deep saucer he always used. Mom always poured coffee into his cup until it spilled over, filling the saucer. He sipped a little from the cup, then set it beside his plate on the oilcloth table cover and picked up the saucer with both hands. Holding it in front of his mouth, he blew lightly on it, then sipped. We called it, "saucering and blowing."

Two more days passed – no Tom.

My neighbor and good buddy Willie came over for the afternoon, even though Mom was not high on my playing with him – he had a sailor's mouth and little respect for the older generation. Willie, a stout, chubby kid, ran his mouth constantly. We were playing with my red wagon in the back yard when he looked around and said, "Somethin' stinks like hell around here."

Mom overheard the comment and thought she smelled something too. About this time Peggy and I noticed the sickly odor coming from the woodpile. Later that afternoon, while Dad chopped wood for the cookstove, he called Mom. "I found Tom," he said, pointing to the woodpile. We gathered, peering through holes in the crisscrossed wood and saw the yellow fur. Clearly, Tom was the source of the odor. "Old Tom's dead," Dad said. "His tomcattin' days are over."

The wretched smell overwhelmed me. I felt sick. My glimpse at the dead cat revealed a bloated body covered with flies. Eager for a breath of fresh air, I went around to the other side of the house, but Mom called. "Leon, get Tom out of there and throw him in that big ditch on the other side of the barn." She left with Dad for the store to buy groceries, leaving me with my sister. "I want that cat out of there when I get back," she said. I learned early to do what I was told. My parents were kind and loving, but when they told you to do something, you did it, there was no room for debate.

They left and I started toward the woodpile, forcing every step. Lots of wood strips had to be moved before the dead cat could be reached. I started digging out the pieces, one at a time. Holding my nose with one hand made the task slow, but I finally got within reaching distance. The urge to run overwhelmed me. I turned, ran a few steps and threw up. I couldn't do it.

Peggy came around the house carrying her favorite doll. I walked over to her and said casually, "How would you like to have a nickel?"

"You don't have one," she said matter-of-factly.

"Yes, I do. Come on, I'll show you."

Peggy followed me into the house and, with some delight, discovered my secret hiding place, the back corner of the bottom dresser drawer. I kept special treasures in a little wooden box made at school, like arrowheads, a piece of fool's gold and *two* nickels.

Nickels meant one thing to my sister and me – a joyful afternoon at the store. We traditionally set aside Saturday afternoons for a family trip to the country store. Peggy and I each got to buy one "thing," usually a bottle of pop, candy bar or maybe a little bag of candy-covered peanuts, each costing a nickel. The adults would sit around and visit. Some of the men played checkers on a homemade board while ladies talked about how many cans of vegetables they had put up.

More often than not, Peggy and I would choose a cold bottle of pop as our one "thing." Nehi strawberry ranked high on our list of preferred drinks, but we usually checked the cooler for new flavors, savoring the moment. Peggy was a tough kid for a seven-year-old, not afraid of anything. After many trips to the store, I learned to use her courage to our advantage. We would finally decide what flavor we wanted and uncap the bottles on the opener attached to the side of the cooler. I suggested we race to see who could drink the whole bottle first. She would jump at the challenge and start chug-a-lugging. I only pretended to drink mine. Her pop was gone within a couple of minutes, and I gloated that I still had mine. That made her mad. After she kicked me a few times, she would go bawling to Mom and Dad, begging for another nickel. I was afraid to do that, remembering their warning on the way to the store, "Only one thing." Peggy knew no fear. She cried and begged and cried and begged until Dad gave her another nickel to shut her up. Then she came prancing to me, holding it high in the air between thumb and finger, giving me the old "Yaa, yaa, yaa." My job was done. All I had to do then was show my face; Dad reached for another nickel before I could point out that Peggy had a second one.

When Peggy saw the two nickels in my secret hiding place, she asked, "What do you want?"

"Get Tom from the woodpile and throw him in the big ditch before Mom and Dad get back," I said, dropping my head.

My little sister walked out the door. I thought for sure I'd struck out but then noticed that she was heading straight for the woodpile. I watched from the kitchen window as she got down on her hands and knees and crawled to that stinkin' cat. How could she do that? She seemed to struggle. I couldn't contain my curiosity and stepped out on the back porch for a closer look. She finally stood up, holding something in her hand.

"The skin come off his front leg," she yelled nonchalantly. I threw up again, but she went back to work. Ten minutes later old Tom lay on the ground beside the woodpile, albeit in several pieces. I ran for a scoop shovel and an old gunnysack. Peggy held the sack while I scooped Tom's remains into it. Intent upon fulfilling her contract, my little sister tried to carry the sack to the big ditch, but couldn't lift it. The old cat must have weighed twenty pounds. We both grabbed the top of the sack, dragged it two hundred yards and heaved it into the big ditch.

"Now, give me my nickel," she said.

"Let's go wash our hands first, then I'll get it," I answered. We stopped at the wash basin outside the kitchen door, where I insisted she scrub her hands with homemade lye soap. All she could think about was the nickel.

I handed her the nickel and started to close the dresser drawer when she said, "I want the other one, too."

"What?"

"If you don't give me the other one, I'm gonna tell Willie and everyone at school what a sissy you are, and Mom and Dad too."

Our parents' Model A Ford stopped in front of the house.

"Here, take it," I said.

Mom's first words: "Leon, is that dead cat out of there?"

"Yep, Mom, all done."

3

MY FIRST HERO

During World War II, my dad worked nights guarding the Powersite Dam twenty miles away near Forsyth. The job paid ten dollars a week. Mom kept us kids quiet during the day while he tried to sleep. We lived in a little house on a forty-acre farm; our nearest neighbors, Will and Sis Blair, lived about a quarter of a mile down the gravel road. Neighbors were few and far between, so we became close to the Blairs. Even though they were pretty old in my young eyes, Mom and Dad always said nice things about them, and that made them okay in my book.

Will Blair was a quiet but fearless man.

Will Blair wore an old floppy-brimmed brown hat and bib overalls. His black hair and eyes, almost covered by bushy eyebrows, might have frightened most children, but at age six I knew him as a kind, grandfatherly man.

His big gnarled hands gripped the double-shovel plow as an old black mule pulled it through garden rows. Will trudged along behind, reins over his neck and under one arm, hands free for guiding the plow. The mule responded to Will's commands: "Haw" told the animal to move left, and "Gee" meant move right. Sometimes he helped my dad in our five-acre strawberry patch. I thought he might be too old to do hard work, but he always managed. Will Blair was a kind, intelligent, old man, respected in the Ozark hill country. His only weakness, in the eyes of his neighbors, was that he and Sis never went to church.

There were no phones in the community. Since Dad worked all night, my mother depended on the Blairs when she had a problem. My mother panicked one early winter evening after my three-year-old sister Peggy found and consumed an entire box of chocolate flavored laxatives. Mom directed me to watch Peggy and ran to the Blairs' home for help. Will and Sis brought her back in their old black 1937 Chevy. They stayed for an hour or two, while Mr. Blair held his massive hand on Peggy's tiny forehead, checking for fever. He finally assured Mom her baby would be fine then went home.

I also remember the night I got the earache, a bad one. I cried for hours until Mom left us alone once again and rushed to the Blairs' for help. She rattled the screen door until the old couple finally awakened. Will explained that he had no medicine but would drive the twenty miles to Forsyth for Dr. Threadgill. Mother refused his generous offer. He said it might help if someone blew warm smoke in my ear.

Upon returning home, Mother rummaged through Dad's dresser drawer until she found a can of Prince Albert smoking tobacco. Like most people back then, Dad rolled his own cigarettes. Mom couldn't locate the little package of tissue-like cigarette paper. My wails grew louder. She improvised by cutting a brown paper bag. I watched, amazed, as my mother poured tobacco onto the heavy brown paper and tried to roll a cigarette. In those days women didn't smoke, especially not cigars, and that is what she had created. She took a wooden match from a box by the cookstove, put the crude makeshift cigar into her mouth and raised the flame to the tip. How she made the paper stick I don't know, but it worked. A big cloud of smoke poured from her mouth. In spite of the intense pain of my earache, I laughed at the sight of Mom puffing that big brown stogie. She didn't think it was funny and said, "Come here." Amid coughs and gags, she held my head gently in her hand, put her mouth close to my ear, and then blew warm smoke. An hour later the pain was gone, and I fell fast asleep.

Like the Blairs, my mom and dad didn't go to church either, until one night someone urged them to go to the Union Flat revival to hear Preacher Sam Stone. Preacher Sam, small and hunchbacked, conducted nightly services in the little white building five miles farther back in the hills. Sam Stone made up for his size with a bellowing voice, parading back and forth, holding an open Bible in his left hand, much as a waiter would carry a tray. Passion spewed from the little man as he preached the gospel, pointing his finger at the small congregation, warning of hellfire and damnation for those not saved by our Savior, the Lord Jesus Christ. Sometimes he would leave the podium and stride down the aisle, delivering the message at closer range to the unrepentant hiding on the back rows.

After he delivered his message and felt he had properly instilled holy terror in the hearts of the unsaved, he asked the congregation to sing hymns during the altar call. Then came the plea to lost souls, "Come forth tonight and be saved." My mom and dad got up and walked past the wood-burning stove to the front of the room while I sat confused and scared on the homemade pew. Brother Stone instructed them to kneel down at the wooden bench that served as an altar while other church members joined him, praying and crying aloud for the Lord to save them. What seemed like hours later, the intonations ceased, and everyone stood up. Tears of joy, congratulations and handshakes replaced loud prayers as the congregation sang "The Old Rugged Cross." My mom and dad would now go to heaven instead of hell, someone told me. After that night we went to church as often as possible.

Later that winter, Brother Sam Stone held another revival at the little Union Flat

Church. One cold Saturday night we went to hear him preach. A fire in the big wood-burning stove standing in the middle of the room warmed the tiny building. Preacher Sam worked up a sweat delivering one of his more powerful sermons. A loud noise at the back of the room caused everyone to turn around. In walked two large young men, hollering as they came. Frank Day, tall and brawny, wore overalls and a big Mackinaw coat. "I can whip any holy rollin' S.O.B. in this room!" he yelled at the top of his voice. His brother, Zack, followed close behind as Frank yanked out a large jackknife with a shiny razor-sharp blade and began whetting it on the hot stove. They were both drunk and kept taking long swigs of corn liquor from a bottle in Frank's hip pocket. We were not holy rollers – we were Southern Baptists, but that made no difference to the Day brothers. Someone there must have done them wrong, or at least they thought so.

Sam Stone stopped preaching. Men, women and children crowded to the sides of the little church. Insults, swearing and brandishing of the big knife continued. One of the male church members darted quickly out the back door, prompting Zack to reposition himself to block any further escapes. The congregation had known the Day boys all their lives, especially Frank, expelled from school in the eighth grade. Trouble followed Frank Day wherever he went. He was a rough-and-tumble fighter whose reputation kept even the most daring men at a distance. He ranted and raved, repeating over and over how he could whip any S.O.B. in the room, chiding the men for not accepting his challenge.

Women and children cried. Men looked at each other as if to say, "Aren't you going to do anything?" Honor and courage surface in men's fantasies as they picture themselves the hero, but when it's time to stare the tiger in the eye, when it's time to act and not just dream, men often find themselves lacking. The Union Flat men faced a twenty-five-year-old bull of a man, six-foot-three, weighing two hundred twenty-five pounds, waving a deadly weapon. A man would have to be crazy to tackle him. Mustering courage, a man tried to talk to Frank in a fatherly manner, only to be told, "Shut up, unless you want to take me on."

The hostages cowered as the bully continued to scream obscenities, words most of the children had never heard. He said he was sick and tired of people "that thinks you are better than the rest of us."

Just then, headlights flashed in the windows and gravel pinged off metal fenders as a car roared up to the front door, horns sounding. Zack opened the door.

"Frank, come here," he said quickly. Both brothers walked out the door, soon followed by most of the church people.

We saw two cars, engines off, headlights on, light flooding the concrete church steps. The driver opened his door and slowly stepped out of the first car, an old 1937 Chevy. Who was it? An old man wearing a floppy-brimmed hat and overalls. Will Blair! My heart thumped. I remember thinking, "What is he doing here?"

"What's goin' on, boys?" he asked, his voice slow and calm.

Before anyone knew what happened, Frank Day jumped off the concrete porch and charged the old man. As if in slow motion, Will Blair sidestepped the young bull, grabbed his knife hand and slammed him to the ground. A dull snap sounded through Frank Day's heavy coat as Will broke his arm, sending the knife sliding across the ground. He grabbed Frank by the nape of the neck and slammed his head repeatedly into the frozen winter ground. Having taken all the fight out of young Day, the old man reached inside his Chevy, pulled out a set of handcuffs and snapped them on his prisoner. Zack had long disappeared, deserting his brother, running off into the dark woods. Deputy Sheriff Will Blair shoved Frank Day into the back seat and slammed the door.

"Go on back to your church services, folks," he said with a smile.

Sam Stone gathered his flock and continued preaching, departing from his interrupted message. He explained to the congregation that while Zack Day whetted his knife on the stove, the preacher had prayed to be delivered. He had no doubt that the Lord had answered his prayer by sending our good neighbor, Will Blair. From that day on, no one criticized Will for not going to church,

And I learned the meaning of the word "hero."

4

DUKE, THE WESTERN HORSE

I saw a horse trailer behind the old pickup parked by our barn as I jumped off the school bus. Dad told me that morning that he had bought a horse and expected him to be delivered in the afternoon. The school day seemed to last forever. We had never owned a horse, and the thought of having my own, like Roy Rogers and Gene Autry, thrilled me.

Mom stood at the front door as my sister and I ran past her toward the barn. She yelled a warning that we should take off our school clothes, but we knew that could wait at least a few minutes.

With five acres of strawberries on top of the rocky hill behind our house and a garden to cultivate, Dad decided a good plow horse would be worth the hundred-dollar investment. He and old John Johnson stood by the trailer looking at the big bay when my sister and I arrived.

"He's a western horse," Dad told us proudly. I didn't know what a western horse was but assumed it to be the kind cowboys rode in the movies. Besides, just the sound "western horse" excited me as I thought about telling my friends. John led him off the trailer into the barnyard where we got a good look.

"His name is Duke," John Johnson said. "He's a western horse," adding value to the old horse he had just sold. "He's good pullin' a garden plow." Duke's ears perked as he surveyed the surroundings. His workhorse body looked as big as an elephant to my sister and me. He snorted, startling us back a few steps. Dad gave John a check and led Duke up to the house where Mom stood in the kitchen door.

I was ten and had ridden horses when spending nights at the home of Stevie Broomfield, a classmate whose father owned horses. Now we had one of our own, and I couldn't wait to get on him.

Dad said we had to be careful with a western horse. Besides, he had to plow the garden and needed to do it right away. He hooked up Duke's harness traces to a singletree and connected it to a double-shovel plow while we watched. He guided Duke into the small garden beside our house. Sweet corn already several inches high and other garden vegetables were just peeking through the soil at the May-afternoon sun. Duke acted up a little bit at first, twisting the traces and stepping on some of Mom's cabbage, but Dad soon had him pulling the plow slowly down the narrow rows.

My sister and I stayed as close to the action as allowed and wondered what Dad was saying. It sounded like "Haw" and "Gee."

"What're you saying to him, Dad?" I hollered.

"I think he's goin' to be a pretty good old plow horse," Dad said. "He knows what haw and gee mean. Watch him bear to the right." Then he said loudly, "Gee!" Duke moved slightly to the right. "Haw!" Dad yelled, and the old horse moved back to the left. They moved down the garden rows, "haws" and "gees" keeping Duke on the right course. Long leather reins from his bridle looped over Dad's head, atop his right shoulder and under his left arm, leaving his hands free for the plow handles.

Daylight lingered as we sat down to supper. Dad unharnessed Duke when he finished plowing and turned him loose in the little pasture outside the kitchen window. Conversation at the table centered on our new horse. Dad pointed out the window, "Look," he said. Duke lay on his side in the grass, attempting to roll over. I guess the drying lather must have been uncomfortable; he was trying to get it off. "A lot of horses can't roll all the way over. If he can turn all the way over, that means he's a good one."

My heart raced as I watched our horse try to prove himself. He lay on his left side for a few seconds, and then with a great heave, threw his feet into the air. It wasn't enough. He rolled back to his left side. I looked at Dad.

"Keep watchin', he'll try again." He did – again, again and again. He never made it. Duke finally stood and shook himself violently. I was disappointed. Dad said, "Don't worry. He might be too tired today from the trailer ride." It made me wonder if he really was a western horse, or if John Johnson had just said that.

Duke turned out to be an excellent plow horse. Sometimes Dad would let me ride the old horse's back as he pulled the plow, but his sweaty lather soaked my overalls. It didn't quite measure up to my visions of Hopalong Cassidy and Randolph Scott.

Interest in Duke waned as we grew accustomed to watching him trudge along garden rows, head hanging low and ears drooping. I tried to ride him a few times, but we had no saddle, and he trotted so hard I thought I would split in two. I think Dad sensed my disappointment. He tried to revive interest by building a heavy wood sled, runners made of two-by-twelve lumber held together by heavy boards nailed across the top. He rigged it so Duke could pull it over any kind of surface. We loved riding the rugged contraption as the old horse pulled the sled over rocky ground, through brushy thickets, even across the small stream running through our farm. Dad used it to haul things too, like manure from the barn to fertilize our garden.

One hot July day, Dad and Duke had been dragging heavy loads of rocks from our pastures and dumping them into a big ditch. After a few hours they were both exhausted and soaked with sweat. Dad tied Duke, still hitched to the sled, to an orchard fence post. He sat down under the big shade tree in our front yard to rest and drink cold water.

"Leon!" he yelled, "Get that cow out of the peach orchard." I grabbed some rocks and started hurling them in her direction, hollering at the top of my voice. The old milk cow paid no attention, but Duke did. He reared high, breaking the reins tied to the fence, pawing the air with his huge hooves. My heart jumped. He looked exactly like Trigger, Roy Rogers' great horse. But Duke didn't stop with rearing; he took off up the hill toward the strawberry patch as fast as he could run, the cumbersome sled flying in the air behind him. The faster he ran, the faster the sled chased, pressing him on to greater speed.

Dad jumped up. Mom and my sister ran out of the house. Ol' Brownie started barking as we listened to Duke tearing through the trees and brush when he passed out of sight. For a couple of minutes we couldn't see Duke, but the thrashing of brush and jangling traces signaled his course. He emerged from the woods far up the hill, heading back toward the house at top speed. Somewhere along the way he stripped the sled, probably running between trees too close together. Now the wooden singletree, still fastened to the traces, was flying up, hitting him on the rump.

I caused the mess by throwing rocks at the old cow and even amid the excitement wondered how Dad was going to handle the situation.

Duke looked like pictures I had seen of the great thoroughbred Man-of-War as he raced down the hill, going faster than ever, trying to outrun the singletree pounding him at every stride. I looked at Dad.

"Sic 'im, Brownie!" Dad yelled. Ol' Brownie loved to be sicked, loved to chase anything, especially old Duke. I was confused. Dad laughed and waved his hat as Duke raced by the house, Ol' Brownie in hot pursuit, barking his head off. Mom was crying, Dad laughing, and I was stunned. Charging down the hill at top speed, Duke accidentally stepped on one of the traces and fell flat, passing gas so loudly you could hear it for a half a mile. He jumped up and took off again, running past the barn, across the hayfield, into the woods on the lower side, and down by the branch.

Everything was quiet. I expected to see him charging back up the hill, but nothing happened. I followed Dad as he walked across the hayfield and into the woods where our horse had disappeared. We found Duke at the very corner of our property facing the fence corner post, trembling so badly you could hear his chains rattle. Dad walked up to him, spoke softly, patted the old horse and took the reins in hand. He turned him around, faced the house, grabbed the harness and jumped on his back. Duke stood still as Dad reached up and broke a small limb off a tree.

"That was a pretty good show, Duke," he said. "You like to run so good, let's try a little more of it." With that, he laid into Duke with his tree limb, sending him tearing through the trees and across the hayfield all the way back to the house. I followed as fast as I could run, arriving about the time Dad was taking off Duke's harness. He led him over to a big tub of cool water and removed the bridle. Duke gulped several gallons and walked away.

At supper that evening, Mom brought a fresh-baked chocolate pie to the table for dessert, my favorite, as I looked out the window. "Dad, look! Old Duke is trying to roll over." Everyone stood up to get a better look. Old Duke made a mighty heave, rolled all the way over, then rolled all the way back again! My sister and I cheered.

Dad smiled, "Told you. He's a western horse! Let's have some chocolate pie."

5

HOT ACORNS & TWENTY-TWO SHELLS

Union Flat School, a few years after the hot acorns incident.

A movable wall divided our little country schoolhouse, which also doubled as a church. Miss Johnson taught grades one through four in the back part. Mr. Hall taught fifth through eighth grades in front. I was in the seventh.

As I jumped off the bus one morning and raced toward the unfenced schoolyard, a cold December wind bent trees and bushes. A clearing of about two acres made up the school parking lot and playground. A cedar thicket formed a wall around the edges of the play area, which served as a magnet for the country schoolchildren. I ran with the other boys toward the thicket, straining to get every possible minute of playtime before Mr. Hall pulled the rope, ringing the big church bell atop the building.

Junior and Tommy Day and I quickly gathered kindling, piled it in the center of the big cedar room and lit it with a wooden match. We boys had brought axes, hatchets and bailing wire to build cedar huts at the beginning of the school year. The fort we had worked on since September resembled a thatched hut, containing one large room ten feet across and a crawl-through door leading to a smaller room. Other boys began showing up, including Raymond Wofford, a large, sullen eighth-grader carrying a big armload of kindling. He threw it on the fire.

"Hey!" Junior yelled, "Whatta you tryin' to do, burn the place down?"

"Shut up," Raymond said. The blaze leapt toward the cedar boughs hanging from the ceiling. "You're a chicken. I ain't afraid."

"That's 'cause you're too stupid," Junior said, looking straight into the larger boy's eyes. "You do that ever' day, and one of these days you're gonna catch this whole place on fire."

Raymond reached into the pocket of his bib overalls and pulled out a handful of twenty-two shells. "Wonder what would happen if I threw these in the fire," he said with a surly smile.

"They'd probably go off and put your eye out," I answered.

Without warning, Raymond threw the handful of live twenty-two cartridges into the crackling fire. We could have run outside, but instead all seven or eight boys dived through the small opening leading to the attached room. I lay face down on the ground to be sure I wouldn't get my eyes put out when the shells started exploding. Tommy dropped beside me, hands covering his eyes. Someone landed on top of me, then someone on him. The pile of boys grew as live ammunition blew, bullets and cartridges whizzing through cedar boughs. Everybody laughed and tried to crawl to the bottom of the pile for protection from the exploding missiles.

The school bell rang as cartridges continued to explode, brass casings whizzing through the cedar-branch roof of our hut. The big school bell sounded louder as Mr. Hall pulled the rope and released it after each clang. Even with bullets zinging all around, we dived through the canvas flap hanging over the backdoor opening and raced toward the little schoolhouse.

We scrambled to our seats before the last clang of the bell.

A large wood-burning stove stood in the center of the schoolroom, scorching those sitting near while those farther away shivered. That same day we put the stove to a new use. Since we often collected acorns from the woods around the school, we decided to roast them on the hot stove. We literally covered the flat castiron top with dozens of acorns that we planned to eat as soon as they roasted, a custom passed down from our forefathers.

Mr. Hall's no-nonsense teaching style quickly settled the class. He handed out assignments to the older kids so he could help fifth- and sixth-graders with reading. Pete Wofford, Raymond's cousin, sat in the double desk beside me. Pete, a handsome kid with naturally curly blond hair, leaned over and whispered, "Did you do them arithmetic problems?"

"Yeah, didn't you?" I asked.

"No, went coon huntin' last night," he said gloomily. He knew Mr. Hall would not be happy.

"You're gonna be in trouble," I said, watching a worried look creep over his face. Then it occurred to me that Pete had a way out. "Why don't you throw up?" I said. We closely guarded the secret that Pete could vomit whenever he wished, and had done so on other occasions when he wanted to go home.

He looked at me a few seconds, pondering the idea, then leaned over and puked. Becky Jane Wilson sat across the aisle, and vomit splashed over her anklets. Mr. Hall rushed to Pete's side. He grabbed the boy's forehead, "You okay, Pete?" he asked nervously. "What's the matter?"

"Dunno," Pete said weakly, his head on the desk. "Must be somethin' I et. Uh-oh, I think I'm goin' to puke again."

"I think you better go home," the teacher said. "Do you feel like walking home?" Pete lived only a mile from school and walked the easy distance every day.

"Yeah, I think I can make it. Maybe somebody should go with me to be sure, like Leon," Pete said weakly.

"Okay, that's a good idea." Mr. Hall was relieved. "Leon, do you want to walk home with Pete, then come right back?"

"Yeah, I guess, but what about class?" I asked, faking concern.

"Don't worry, this will be excused," Mr. Hall said.

Pete and I walked out the door and across the playground slowly, dragging our feet while still in sight of the school. As soon as we followed the path into the trees, we whooped and hollered, rolling on the ground, laughing. Pete had a pouch of tobacco and some roll-your-own papers, so we sat on a big log and rolled cigarettes.

"This is Dad's pipe tobacker," he said. "It's so strong it'll take the hide off your tongue if you ain't careful." We made big, fat, awkward cigarettes and lit them with wooden matches. The last time we had smoked, Pete's older brother made fun of us, "You don't even inhale. Ain't even real smokin'," he said. This time we decided we would really smoke. I took a big puff and sucked it into my lungs but coughed it up each time. Soon we both were coughing and wheezing. Dizziness turned into sick stomachs and we both vomited – for real. We threw our cigarettes down, and Pete headed home while I straggled back to school. I was pale when I walked in and sat at my desk next to the hot stove. Mr. Hall was looking at me when I felt it coming. I leaned over and threw up in the aisle, splashing Becky Jane's anklets again.

"My land!" Mr. Hall said as he rushed to my side. "Did you catch something from Pete already?"

I put my head on the desk and didn't answer.

"Stay right there," he said. "Keep your head down for a while."

One of the acorns on the hot stove popped, spraying shell across the room.

"Okay, that's enough with these acorns," Mr. Hall said to everyone. "I want those acorns off the stove now!"

Big Raymond Wofford didn't like the idea. "How come?" he asked, obviously agitated.

"Because they get hot and bust; one might explode and put someone's eye out, so get 'em off – now."

The acorns were hot, but each boy managed to grab his own acorns or swipe them off onto the floor as Raymond mumbled under his breath.

"Time for English," Mr. Hall announced. "I want the seventh- and eighth-graders to write three sentences using active verbs. Do it now, then we'll trade papers and read them before recess. I'm going to work with the fifth and sixth grades on reading."

Fifteen minutes later Mr. Hall said, "Okay, trade papers with your neighbor."

Mr. Hall told Becky Jane to read first. She had Doug Iverson's paper – not the brightest boy in class.

"I seen a squirrel and shot its brains out," she read from Doug's paper.

"Stop right there," the teacher said. "Now, class, what's wrong with that sentence?"

Johnnie Roberts threw his hand up.

"Yes, Johnnie."

"Doug ain't never shot no squirrel in his life. He's lyin'."

"Am not lyin'!" Doug quickly defended himself.

"That's not the point, Johnnie," Mr. Hall said. "You used the wrong verb form, Doug. You should have said, 'I *saw* a squirrel,' not 'I *seen.*'"

"Leon, whose paper do you have?" he asked.

"Raymond's."

"Read his first sentence," Mr. Hall instructed.

I looked at the paper, then glanced at Raymond. He wore a thin smile.

"Acorns don't bust, you crazy fool," I read, loud and clear.

Chuckles rippled across the schoolroom.

Mr. Hall looked at Raymond, who looked straight back, smiling. "You think that's funny, Raymond?"

"Yeah," said the big eighth-grader.

"Okay, if it's so funny, I think all the students would like to see it in writing. So, while they are at recess, and for the rest of the day, Raymond, I want you to stand at the blackboard and write that sentence five hundred times."

Mr. Hall dismissed the class for recess. Raymond leaned over my desk and asked, "How did Pete learn you to puke?"

6

MY COUSIN BOBBY RAY

I don't know what it was about my first cousin Bobby Ray Maggard that caused me to idolize him. I was about ten or eleven years old when Mother and Dad took me for one of our regular Sunday-afternoon drives after church, ending up at Bobby Ray's house. Hog-killin' time, and Aunt Goldie, Bobby Ray's mother, invited us over for a Sunday dinner of fresh pork. His dad had butchered a hog that week with help from neighbors.

The same neighbors shared the fresh meat. It was especially valued since no one had freezers or refrigerators in the pre-electricity days in Southwest Missouri's Ozark hills. Fresh hog meat not eaten right away or shared with family and neighbors was canned in glass fruit jars or cured and hung in the smokehouse.

Bobby Ray Maggard was my idol; in my eyes, he could do no wrong.

The Maggards lived in a little white house in the country sitting on a high spot beyond the crossing of a small creek. I saw Bobby Ray jump off the front porch as our Model A Ford slowed to cross the low-water bridge. Mom, who thought Bobby rambunctious, warned me not to scuff up my new shoes or get my church clothes dirty. By the time our car stopped in the narrow dirt driveway, Bobby was jumping up and down, eager for a playmate. Bobby's old collie dog, Mange, lay on the front porch. He looked mean to me, and I was always a little afraid of him, especially since I never saw him wag his tail. I threw open the car door and raced headlong for the creek with Bobby.

A loud yell from my dad stopped me in my tracks. "You better remember what your maw said about them new shoes! If you get 'em wet or scuff 'em up, I'll have to whoop you!"

"Same goes for you, Bobby," his dad shouted, just to keep rules consistent, I suspected.

Looking back on our relationship, I think Bobby Ray operated the same way I've since seen many powerful men and women do in all walks of life, in business, politics or law – he simply assumed power and authority. He wasn't bigger or stronger than I, but I followed him everywhere, never doubting for a minute anything he told me. He was all-powerful as far as I was concerned.

I went to Bradleyville School and played on the elementary basketball team. Bobby

Ray, living farther back in the hills, went to a little country school that didn't have a team. Though we lost most of our games, I remember daydreaming about how good we would be if Bobby Ray could play on our team. Heck, he didn't even know how to play basketball. But my view of him convinced me that with him on the court, we would never lose another ballgame. Maybe it was his undaunted outlook on life, confident and assertive approach, or his matter-of-fact pronouncements that seemed invincible. If Bobby said it, that's the way it was. I just could not imagine his losing at anything.

That Sunday, we charged toward the little stream teaming with crawfish and minnows. Bobby had set what he called a "minner" trap to catch minnows for fish bait. I glanced over my shoulder and saw my dad and Bobby's dad standing on the front porch, visiting and looking our direction. A sheet of clear water flowed over the concrete slab, providing a solid footing for traffic to cross the stream. Bobby motioned me to follow as he jumped from stone to stone across the little stream. We made it all the way across by jumping from one flat stone to the other.

The crystal-clear creek ran swiftly, lapping over edges of the stepping stones. The water smelled fresh and clean, gurgling and buffeting into rocks, fallen tree trunks and the concrete slab. Brightly colored autumn leaves, newly departed from overhanging limbs, decorated the flowing stream.

Bobby Ray crossed ahead of me and looked back as I prepared to jump from the last rock to the bank, a longer distance than between the other steps. I looked down at my new shoes, over my shoulder at our dads on the porch and jumped. Made it, just barely, but Bobby Ray had to grab my hand to save me from falling back into the water.

Upstream from our crossing lay a quiet pool of shimmering water at least a hundred yards long. Big willow trees on each side of the creek bowed toward each other, forming an arch and casting shade over the cool water. We entertained ourselves for quite a while skipping rocks across the glassy smooth surface. "The secret," my cousin said, "is finding a good skippin' rock, thin and round." You threw it sidearm to see how many skips you could get on the water. Bobby won the contest – *seventeen* skips with an especially good rock. I didn't mind losing to him; in fact, I *expected* to lose to Bobby Ray.

Dad hollered for us to come to dinner, so we headed back to the crossing. I decided to go first. Bobby said, "You have to get a running start so you can jump to that first rock." I stood on the bank, measured the distance with my eyes and decided how far to back up for my run. Thorny blackberry bushes pricked my backside as I stood ready to make the charge. I looked up at the little house on the hill and saw our fathers watching, then took off and jumped. I was airborne before I realized the flat rock was wet and probably slick. I did a touch-and-go, both feet landing on the slick rock for an instant, then my backside splashed into the creek. Even suspended above the water, I cast a quick glance to the porch. Dad was watching.

By the time I rolled over and got to my feet, not only were my new shoes soaked, but so were my church clothes, from head to foot. I turned to Bobby on the bank. He seemed disappointed, knowing I was in trouble.

"Well, you're gonna get a whoopin', so we might as well both get one." He made a giant leap directly into the deepest part, intentionally rolling around to be sure he was completely soaked too.

Dad hated whipping me anytime, and seldom did, but I don't think Bobby's dad was bothered all that much with laying it on his son. He probably did it about once a day. Dad took hold of my arm and whacked me four or five times across the butt. It didn't hurt but prompted me into little snubs of a cry. Jim Maggard wasn't so easy on Bobby Ray, hitting him harder and more times, but my cousin didn't shed a tear. Admiration for my cousin moved up another notch.

The dinner table was piled high with fresh hog meat. At that time I had never heard the word "pork." Aunt Goldie rounded off the meal with mashed potatoes, green beans, applesauce, and my favorite dessert, chocolate pie. Bobby and I ate as fast as our parents would allow, so we could get back to playing. Mom and Aunt Goldie found a pair of Bobby's old bib overalls and worn-out shoes for me to wear, and we headed for the woods across the road.

Bobby Ray knew where squirrels had a nest on an overhanging limb of a big oak tree. He promised me there was a big red squirrel in it, and if we could hit the nest with a rock, the squirrel would jump to the ground where old Mange would kill it. So we went to work, hunting good throwin' rocks, hurling them at the nest. The nest, made of twigs and leaves, was about twelve inches across. Old Mange stood too close to me for comfort, and I kept moving away. Bobby noticed and said, "You don't have to worry about him, unless he sets down and starts scratchin'. Then, you better watch out. That means he's getting ready to have a mad fit."

That did it. I could no longer concentrate on hitting the squirrel's nest. That dog had to be watched. Bobby kept firing missiles at the nest, even hit it a couple of times, but no squirrel emerged.

Old Mange sat down, and I froze in my tracks. Then the old dog lifted his hind leg and started frantically scratching his neck.

"Uh-oh! Here he goes!" Bob yelled, "A mad fit's comin'."

I headed for the nearest tree. A small limb jutted out from the trunk a foot above the ground, not big enough to support me, but in my panic I tried to use the puny limb as a step so I could reach a larger one higher up. Every time I tried to push myself up by stepping on the limb, it bent to the ground, giving me no advantage. The old dog scratched faster and Bobby Ray climbed another tree, yelling louder, "Hurry, he's about to go mad."

I kept stepping on the limb faster and faster, crying and clawing the trunk of the hickory tree. Fear paralyzed my mind and body, rendering me helpless, petrified.

Suddenly, old Mange stood up and walked off toward the house, losing interest in the abandoned squirrel hunt. I could feel warm wetness – I had peed on Bobby's overalls. My cousin laughed and came over to give me a hand. We walked back to the house without saying much.

Seeing I had been crying and had wet my pants, Bobby Ray's dad asked me what happened.

"Nothin'," I said, not wanting to get Bobby in trouble, but his dad knew him too well.

"Bobby Ray, come here," he said, pulling off his big leather belt. "I'm tired of talkin' to you." This time he meant business and really laid the leather to his son. To my surprise, Bobby cried.

A few minutes later we were playing again, throwing rocks at pop bottles, our parents back inside the house.

"He hit you pretty hard with that belt, didn't he?" I said.

"Nah, didn't even hurt."

"How come you bawled like a calf then?" I asked.

"So he'd stop."

7

THE BOOGER MAN

My Uncle Shade, Dad's brother, delighted in telling stories to children. Scary tales were followed by nightmares keeping us awake all hours of the night. He was a big, jolly, fat man, weighing 350 pounds. No matter how much his stories terrified us, the next time we got together the kids gathered around Uncle Shade, asking him to tell another scary story.

His youngest son, and my favorite cousin, Eddie, never got used to his dad's stories, which scared him more than any of us. Uncle Shade always talked about how the Booger Man would get you if you didn't behave, how he was always hiding behind a bush or around the corner. Billy Pierce personified the Booger

Eddie Combs feared Billy Pierce, the Booger Man.

Man to Eddie more than anyone. While still a toddler, Eddie screamed in terror the first time he ever saw the old man with a long scraggly beard covering almost his entire face. It hung down to mid-chest. His beady black eyes and the tobacco-stained hash mark representing his mouth stood out against the gray beard. Brushy eyebrows hung down almost covering his eyes, and long hairs protruded from his nostrils. An old floppy black hat sat atop a mass of long iron gray hair that blended with his beard. His voice was loud and gravelly.

"If you don't do what I tell you, I'll turn you over to Billy Pierce," Uncle Shade would say, then laugh as Eddie cowered in fear. Billy Pierce *was* the Booger Man as far as Eddie was concerned. His dad told him that Billy had a dark, wet basement full of little kids he had captured. The kids were tied and got nothing to eat except spinach and green beans, according to Uncle Shade.

One day Uncle Shade and Aunt Laura brought Eddie, his brothers and sister to my parents' country store in the rural community of Union Flat. Loafers sat around the potbellied stove, playing checkers, whittling and talking.

"Howdy," Uncle Shade said, always friendly and in a good mood.

Eddie and I immediately headed out the door to play. Both eight years old, we relished every minute together and especially loved it when Uncle Shade and family stayed all night. We could run wild, and I could get away with all sorts of things with Mom, at least until they left for home the next day. Sometimes while they were there, she would grab my arm, pull me close and hiss in my ear, "You just wait 'til they're gone."

Eddie and I played until we tired, then decided to go in the store to see if we could talk our parents out of a bottle of pop. We were coming in the store's back door, when suddenly I heard Eddie holler. He ran backward a few steps, turned and disappeared behind the feed house.

I followed. "What's the matter?"

He was crying, "I seen *him*. He's – he's in there," he said, hunkered down behind the building, gnawing his knuckles.

"Who?" I asked.

"Ol Billy Pierce. He seen me too – was lookin' right at me."

Eddie wouldn't go back into the store until his mom came looking for him. "Time to go home," she said, assuring Eddie that Billy Pierce had left an hour ago.

Uncle Shade's family didn't spend that night with us, but we talked his parents into letting Eddie stay over. Our home was the three back rooms of the store building. We played in the woods until Mom called us for supper. Afterward, we sat on the floor close to our big RCA console radio, listening to our favorite programs: *Jack Armstrong, the All American Boy; Gangbusters,* and *Lum and Abner.*

"Time for bed," Mom said. "Your dad's takin' the truck to Springfield for a load of feed in the morning, so we'll have to get up early, and tomorrow's a school day."

The school bus always picked up my sister and me before daylight in winter, so we were used to getting up early, but it seemed like the middle of the night when Mom told Eddie and me to hit the floor on that cold morning. We jerked on our overalls, grabbed shoes and socks and ran to the front of the building. Dad already had a roaring fire in the store's wood stove. He had taken the truck to pick up some farmer's cow to haul to the Springfield stockyards. Sometimes farmers rode with him to take care of business in the big city.

The sound of dishes and pots and pans and the aroma of frying bacon came from the kitchen as Mom prepared breakfast.

"Wanna throw darts?" I asked Eddie, trying to squeeze a few more minutes of play before his visit ended.

I hung an old dartboard on the Arm & Hammer baking soda shelf next to the stove. We had four darts with worn feather quills.

"I'll go first," I said. "Whoever has the most points when Mom makes us come to breakfast, wins." It was still pitch-dark outside and, the winter wind howled.

"Okay," Eddie said.

Eddie was pretty good and was well ahead of me, which was a little upsetting.

"You're not standing behind the line," I accused. "You've got to stand all the way behind that dark board on the floor, almost with your back against the front door."

"Okay." He stood behind the dark board, back almost touching the big glass window.

The next dart hit the bull's-eye. I dropped my head. I'd never catch him.

Eddie smiled as he raised the second dart, eyes glued to the bull's-eye. The door behind him rattled loudly. He turned around. Six inches away from him, a face pressed against the dark window: a horrifying sight.

Wild eyes and a woolly face, framed by the blackness of predawn, stared into the dimly lit store. Billy Pierce. Eddie paled, turned toward me, eyes wide and mouth open, speechless. He dropped to his knees as Billy rattled the door again, harder this time. That was enough to bring Eddie to life. Both his hands flew over his head. He ran screaming past me, yelling, "The Booger Man, the Booger Man."

I let Billy in.

"Where's your dad?" he asked. "I'm s'posed to ride to Springfield with him."

8

THE GALLOPIN' GOOSE

The two-story building in the foreground served as a church on the ground floor and classrooms for grades one through eight on the second floor.

Miss Lucy tried to quiet the class as twenty-eight kids squirmed and wiggled in their seats on the first day of school. She taught 'readin', 'ritin' and 'rithmetic to grades one through eight.

Brownbranch School occupied the second floor of Caney Church. A large wood stove, located in the center, heated the single room. Pupils pulled chairs in a circle around the stove on especially cold days. The kids knew Miss Lucy as an old maid with no children of her own, but a woman who dealt harshly with misbehavior.

I liked school and looked forward to the first day of the school year. I was one of only two eighth-graders, the other being a beautiful "new" girl, Mariah Powers, sitting in the desk-chair across the aisle. Her parents had moved into our village of Brownbranch a week before school started. Her dad worked for Mr. Dawson, the richest farmer in the county, who also provided a house for the Powers family.

Mariah's white teeth gleamed as she cast a quick smile my way, flaming red hair falling in curls over her shoulders. She was prettier than the other girls and certainly filled the homemade cotton print dress, which was shorter than most. A sash, tied in a bow at the small of her back, emphasized her slender waist. The new girl filled out the front of her dress, making it appear her mother had forgotten to allow for "filling."

I wasn't the only boy who noticed the new girl. Ronnie, Billy and Russell all glanced her way, then toward me as if to ask, "Whatta you think?" Miss Lucy soon got everyone's attention by raising her voice a few levels, demanding all eyes. Starting with first-graders, she assigned seats, little ones in front, eighth-graders on the back row. Mariah's presence and the attention she was getting from the boys had not gone unnoticed by our teacher.

"We have a new classmate this year, boys and girls," she said, looking at Mariah with a semi-smile. "Dear, would you like to tell everyone your name?"

All eyes turned to the pretty eighth-grader. To my surprise, she stood calmly, smiled, and said in a strong feminine voice, "My name's Mariah Powers, and I came here from Iowa." Then she looked around the room, continued smiling, and started to sit.

"Tell us, Mariah," Miss Lucy said, "what are your hobbies?"

Standing erect again, hands clasped loosely in front, Mariah answered, "I like to play baseball and basketball. And I like to go hunting and fishing."

Stunned silence followed. Boys giggled, and the girls looked puzzled, probably thinking, "A girl playing ball, hunting, fishing?" Ronnie laughed, and I started to join in when the teacher spoke sharply, "Enough!" Turning to Mariah, she said, "Dear, you may take your seat. I'm sure all the children welcome you to our school."

Recess – the best part of school – arrived at 10 a.m. We all rushed headlong down the wooden stairs to the playground, about an acre of fairly level ground between the school and Caney Creek. We called the game baseball, but the ball consisted of rubber taken from an old tire tube, wrapped in twine from feed sacks. It made a pretty good ball with lots of life, if you took time to wrap it tightly. We had no real bats; most kids made their own. Mine, a four-foot long one-by-four oak board with the handle area hewn down so I could grip it, was pretty heavy and would really drive the ball if I hit it squarely.

We wasted no time – recess went by fast – so I appointed myself one of the captains and Ronnie Dunn the other. Captains chose sides after flipping a coin to see who went first. I flipped a nickel and told Ronnie to call it. The loser batted first.

"Heads," he yelled.

"It's tails," I said. "I'll take Russell."

Other than myself, I considered Russell Selvidge the best ballplayer in school. We allowed only boys in the sixth grade and up to play, a total of eleven to choose from, or five each, plus Doug Stillwell. Doug always struck out and could never catch anything, so he was never chosen. Girls didn't play ball. They jumped rope or played jacks or drop-the-handkerchief. Russell walked proudly to stand by me. Ronnie took his brother Billy; then we alternated choosing until each team had five boys. We started to take the field.

"You can have Doug," I said to Ronnie.

"Go down by the creek, Doug," Ronnie ordered, "in case someone hits a ball down there."

"I want to play." Everyone stopped and looked at the new girl, standing with hands on hips, not smiling. Mariah didn't frown and she was not about to cry. Her blue eyes blazed directly at me, feet planted firmly.

I looked at Ronnie, then turned to her and said, "Girls don't play ball here."

"I'm goin' to," she said firmly.

"You can have her," I told Ronnie and proceeded to take the field. I was also the self-appointed pitcher, so I took position on the little spot with no grass that we called the pitcher's mound. Ronnie grabbed his bat and stepped in. We pitched underhanded and didn't call balls and strikes, except when the batter swung and missed. A "good" pitcher only had to get the ball in the strike zone so the batter could hit it. Each team had a pitcher, catcher, first baseman and two fielders—the fielders played wherever they thought best. If a batter got to first base, the game became "cross-out," meaning if he passed more than halfway to the next base, you only had to throw the ball in front of the player across the baseline to get him out.

Standing at home plate, a player looked directly at Caney Creek, about two hundred feet away, flowing from left to right. If a ball landed in the creek, it counted as an automatic home run. Few kids hit the ball that far, although some fathers had shown us it could be done.

Ronnie held the bat on his shoulder and waited for my pitch. I looped one as near the fat strike zone as I could and he whacked it over my head to center field. Russell caught it on first bounce. Ronnie was already at first.

I turned to face the next batter. Mariah! There she stood, sunlight gleaming off her red hair, big smile, bat on shoulder, crouching over the plate. I didn't know what to do. No girl ever played ball with us, unless we let her run down balls in the outfield. Certainly none had ever been allowed to bat. I looked at Ronnie. He shrugged and looked back helplessly.

"You gonna pitch, or what?" she yelled.

I pitched, but the ball hit the ground in front of her. I was shaken.

"Hey, Buster, that the best you can do?" She'd called me "Buster!" What she needs is to be struck out, I thought. That'll cool her down. So I pitched as fast as I could. She swung and missed an inside ball. My catcher smiled and threw the ball back. "Strike one," I yelled loudly, so everyone could hear, then sent another pitch flying, this time to the outside.

"*Wham!*" The bat connected with blazing speed, sending the ball zooming high over my head so fast I lost track of it for a moment. I watched it soar over the outfield, over Doug's head, and splash into the swift waters of Caney Creek. The new girl whooped and shouted, holding hands high in the air as she rounded the bases. Other girls yelled and cheered, including Miss Lucy.

Recess ended. We entered the classroom with a different view of the new girl. Maybe it was a fluke, I thought. Maybe she just got lucky. During lunch and afternoon recess we put her through some tests.

At noon, after gobbling down our peanut-butter-and-jelly sandwiches, I suggested a rock-throwing contest. All the boys gathered good throwin' rocks. I watched from the corner of my eye as the new girl also picked up rocks. *That's what I thought – she thinks she can outthrow the boys.* I got everyone lined up behind me, facing Caney Creek, then drew a line that couldn't be stepped over without a foul. I went first. I had a good round rock, exactly right for distance. Everyone backed up to give me a little runnin' room so I could put everything I had behind the throw without going over the foul line. It was a good throw; the rock sailed over Caney, landing in tall weeds on the other side. Other boys took turns, but only Ernie Metcalf's throw outdistanced mine. Ernie, small and sinewy, much to my dismay, always managed to throw farther than I. Behind Ernie, last in line, stood the new girl. Ernie walked over, wearing a big grin, bumped me with his elbow and said under his breath, "Let her try to beat that."

Mariah took her time. She bent forward, arms swinging like a baseball pitcher getting ready to go into his windup. She looked straight ahead for a minute, then at Ernie and me and smiled. She hauled off and let fly a monstrous throw, not like a girl, but a man. The rock cleared Caney Creek, way past mine and Ernie's, striking the hillside twenty yards beyond. Again the girls cheered, but the boys were silent.

I couldn't concentrate in class after lunch. What kind of girl was this? At recess that afternoon, I decided to give her the ultimate test – a footrace. I had always been, by far, the fastest runner in school, so, figuring she would follow, I led the boys to a big elm about a hundred yards from the well pump in front of the school. We would race, I announced, two at a time. We formed two lines. I was last in one line; the new girl last in the other. She and I would race. The boys ahead stood erect, waiting for Kay Dunn to yell, "Go!" We didn't know anything about getting down in a crouch the way track runners did, so we just stood, tense and ready, until we heard the command.

My heart pumped so hard I could feel an artery throbbing in my neck before we advanced to the front of the line. She smiled at me, relaxed and ready. Finally, everyone else had run. They stood at the finish line watching the girl and me. Kay stood off to the side, hand raised to give the start signal. Mariah Powers continued to smile. I was dry-mouthed and grim-faced.

"Ready! Set! Go!" Kay yelled. We were off. I got a split-second jump on her, head back, running like the wind, accustomed to running off and leaving my competitors. Out of the corner of my eye I could see her edging up, red hair flying. I strained every muscle for an extra bit of speed, but she gradually edged up beside me. I could see my friends ahead by the well pump, yelling, urging me on, but the redheaded girl, frilly dress flying in the wind, crossed the line inches ahead of me.

It took a while for boys from male-dominated families to accept reality – this girl was stronger, faster, and a better athlete than any boy in school. She lived about half a mile from our little village of Brownbranch, where my mother and father owned the country store. The new girl ran everywhere she went, prompting Truman Dixon to tag her "The Gallopin' Goose." Something had to be done to put this girl in her place, even if it meant labeling her with an unattractive nickname.

Mariah's achievements targeted her for scorn, but the kids liked her. She was extremely attractive, constantly smiling, friendly to everyone, and not at all bigheaded. It was hard to dislike a very pretty girl who could outperform boys, especially a girl who certainly didn't look like a boy.

The school year zoomed by. We found ourselves with the coming summer to enjoy before going on to high school at Bradleyville. Ronnie, Billy, Russell and I worked long and hard, building a raft like the one in *The Adventures of Tom Sawyer.* Using Dad's crosscut saw, we cut down trees, laid logs side by side, then nailed them together with one-by-fours. We finished one evening just before dark and decided to launch our craft the next day; no sleep for me that night. The raft belonged to us boys; we did not let Mariah help us, although she did lots of watching. She came the next morning to watch when we pushed and shoved the heavy craft toward the creek. Too heavy; we couldn't move it. We finally let her help. With her, the task seemed easy; the raft slid down the bank into the deep water, and kept on going straight to the very bottom! We were stunned. All that work so we could float on it, take our reels and rods, even build fires on it. But it lay at the bottom in ten feet of clear water, motionlessly. No one spoke. We looked at each other, then started up the hill to the store. I turned, walked away from the others and sat on a big log, hanging my head. I heard a noise and looked up. There she stood, hands clasped in front, the same way she stood in class that first day of school. She was crying, silently, big tears rolling down her cheeks.

"I'm so sorry," she said quietly. "Maybe you shouldn't have used green logs."

I motioned for her to sit by me. She stepped forward timidly and sat close, but not touching. I looked into her eyes and saw understanding and love. I kissed her. My first kiss, a wet kiss, wet with her tears.

9

THE WRESTLERS

We moved to Brownbranch in 1948. Dad and Mom bought the only store in the country village. I was thirteen and became fast friends with an elderly, one-eyed neighbor named Amy Floyd. Amy always wore a smile and showed me the best fishing holes in Beaver Creek. He took the Springfield daily paper and listened to the radio news a lot; he knew more than most people, especially about sports.

Together, Amy and I listened on his squawking radio to the championship fights of my hero Joe Louis. One night, just after Louis had knocked out an opponent, Amy turned to me and made a startling statement that almost knocked me out: "You know he's a nigger, don't you?"

"Who?" I asked, afraid of his answer.

"Joe Louis," he answered, matter-of-factly. I had never known Amy to make a mistake about sports, but how could he possibly be right about this? No one

Amy Floyd was a kind gentleman and an authority, I thought, on professional wrestling.

on the radio had ever said anything about Joe Louis being colored. I didn't believe him, but knowing I had no ammunition for an argument, I kept quiet.

Professional wrestling was not on the radio in those days; at least it never reached Brownbranch, but Amy told me all about it. He had been to the matches in person many times and told me straight out: "You've never seen anything until you have seen a *real* fight between them big, mean wrestlers." His comment was especially interesting because I liked to wrestle with boys in school and usually beat everyone my size. Amy's vivid tales of macho men destroying opponents in the ring spurred fantasies about my own potential and caused me to flex my muscles in front of the bedroom mirror.

One day Amy calmly made a suggestion that set my heart racing. "Why don't we go to the Shrine Mosque in Springfield Saturday night and see Gorgeous George?" Gorgeous George, the world champion wrestler! In person? I doubted if Mom and Dad would let me go, but to my surprise they had no problem; Amy was a solid citizen.

On a January evening we gassed up Amy's old '39 Chevy at our store. Dad only charged Amy half price since I was going with him to the Shrine Mosque. The old man with one good eye slid the seat up close to the steering wheel, pulled his hat down low over his forehead, like a bull rider, gripped the steering wheel with both hands and hung on for dear life. The old car lurched forward in fits and starts; we were on our way. Traveling at thirty miles an hour, I thought we would never get to the nearest paved road, twenty-five miles away at Sparta. We crawled over the hills and curves of the graveled Highway 125.

Darkness overtook us about the time we hit the good road, and I soon noticed my companion had difficulty dealing with the bright headlights of oncoming cars. Nevertheless, we approached the outer limits of Springfield, the largest city I had ever seen, and until that night, only during daytime when Dad took me with him to haul feed and groceries for his store. What a spectacle at night! Brownbranch had had electricity for only a couple of years, and here before me lay more lights than I could believe existed.

Amy found the Shrine Mosque and a parking place, a remarkable achievement considering he was half-blind and driving at night in a strange place. I started to open the door when he told me to sit tight while he took care of some very important business. He calculated the cost of admission, two hot dogs, and two bottles of pop, left that amount in his billfold and folded the remaining twenty-three dollars, which he then slid all the way down his high sock to the sole of his foot. "That," he said, "will fool any mugger that tries to get my money." I marveled at his worldliness and decided then and there to use the same trick if I ever had that much extra money and happened to be in a strange place.

I had seen pictures of the steps leading up the front of the U. S. Capitol in Washington. That's what the entrance of the gigantic Shrine Mosque reminded me of as we mounted the steps. The lobby was alive with people, laughing, talking, and music blaring over loudspeakers. I grew a little dizzy and was distracted trying to absorb everything at once when I realized Amy was tugging at my arm, asking if I wanted a hot dog and bottle of pop. I thought of Joe Louis the second I saw the colored vendor, the first time I had ever seen anyone other than an Anglo-Saxon. Of course I wanted the hot dog, I said, staring at the colored man. He smiled, said thank you in a deep resonant voice, and went about his business. Maybe it's not so bad – the colored business about Joe Louis – after all, I thought. What difference did it make? Why had I been so upset? Just because I had always visualized one thing and discovered something totally different? That Negro man seemed just like everyone else, except for the color of his skin.

The inside of the arena appeared larger than I had imagined. We didn't have a gymnasium at Bradleyville School, but I had played in the one at Forsyth and figured you could put about a dozen high school gyms inside this place and still have room left over. "We've got good seats," Amy said. They were on the very top row. It would be easy to get to the rest room and get out when it was over. Again, I was impressed that old Amy had thought of everything. The place was filled with thousands of rowdy fans, already yelling and booing, throwing junk at the two wrestlers just entering the ring. From where we sat they looked rather small, way down in the center of the arena. Amy pulled a telescope from his coat pocket, focused it on the ring, then handed it to me.

"That one with the long blond hair is Gorgeous George," he said. "The other guy is a real jerk." Leave it to Amy to get a telescope instead of field glasses, I thought. Why have two things to look through when you have only one eye? As I watched the wrestlers through the scope, I could clearly see that George was a really nice guy, standing quietly in his corner while the other guy showed off his muscles and pranced around the ring. He even threw some stuff back at fans, making me a little nervous because I could see some of the crowd close to the ring acting really crazy.

Even before the match started, the fracas began. The referee introducing the wrestlers must have said something that aggravated George's opponent because he just hauled off and knocked him down. The referee knocked down on purpose! I was shocked and, frankly, scared. What in the world would happen next? Amy was agitated more than I had ever seen him but leaned over to me and yelled in my ear, "Watch George. He'll get him." And he did. The Great Gorgeous George tore into that jerk and threw him to the floor again and again as the crowd roared. He gave him a pretty bad beating for a while, until the referee got up enough nerve to stop them, for a rest I guess. As they were resting, one of the loudmouths at ringside called the jerk a name or something and threw a tomato at him, which really made him mad. He started crawling through the ropes to go after the guy.

Let me tell you, I was ready to leave. It was obvious to me the place was going to turn into a serious riot. Chairs started flying, uniformed guards got into the fray, and sirens went off. I was really impressed since I had never heard a real siren, except on the radio. Amy was on his feet, screaming at the jerk, and once again I appreciated our "good" seats, at least a hundred yards from the action. Finally, to my great relief, the police were able to get the wrestlers in, and the fans out, of the ring.

George proceeded to whip the miserable numbskull unmercifully while we cheered wildly. Just as Amy had said, we were among the first out the door when it was over. What an experience. I was sure the guys at school wouldn't believe me when I told them how close we'd come to a real disaster.

Heavy fog hung over the road during the long, dark drive home. Amy was seventy-five years old and had only one eye. I was thirteen and had no driver's license. The old car's headlights were dim, without fog lights, but with the windshield wipers going and both of us working together, we made it to Garrison, only thirteen miles from home. Amy stopped in the middle of the road, or wherever we were; it was impossible to tell.

"You can drive, can't you?" he said.

"Yes," I answered. Dad taught me to drive on a Model A when I was ten.

"Then you're gonna have to see if you can get us home," my good friend said. He scooted over to my side and I walked around to the driver's seat. With visibility about zero, I rolled down the window, stuck my head out, and drove five miles an hour all the way through Bradleyville to Brownbranch, without ever seeing another car.

Two big thrills in one night were almost too much. The Shrine Mosque experience still lives in my memory and will forever, but so will the fact that my friend Amy trusted a boy to drive him home.

When I got to the store after school on Monday afternoon, the checker players and loafers had already heard about our trip. I couldn't believe it when Ike Whitaker, one of the better checker players, made a snide remark about wrestling *being fake!* I just laughed. Old Ike might have been a good checker player, but he obviously knew nothing about professional wrestling. If he could see – just one time – what we saw, he would know the truth. I realized then and there, if you want to know the truth, you have to see for yourself.

10

Ol' Brownie

I loved Ol' Brownie, my reddish part-hound dog, as much as he loved to chase rabbits. He was my constant companion from age twelve to seventeen. "Good" dogs in my youth treed squirrels, possums, or coon. Rabbit-chasing dogs were scorned and ridiculed. Who wanted rabbits? And if a dog chased rabbits over all other forms of prey, he'd never be considered a "good" dog again. Unfortunately, the community judged Ol' Brownie the world's worst dog due to his eagerness to

We lived in some rented rooms of the big white house in the background. This picture was taken from the approximate spot where Ol' Brownie died.

chase rabbits from morning to night. If measured by how much he loved what he did, how many rabbits he caught (not an easy game), how hard he worked at it, Brownie would have been reckoned one of the better dogs on the planet. He could leap tall fences at full stride. Other dogs might lose a rabbit if it ran through a woven wire fence; Ol' Brownie actually gained ground with a gigantic jump over the barrier, often almost landing on top of his prey.

I never gave up trying to break Ol' Brownie from running after rabbits. One winter day, watching him chase a scared hare in the snow near our barn, I yelled and scolded as he bore down hard on the terrified animal. As he was about to chomp it with his strong jaws, the rabbit stopped suddenly and dove into the snow; Brownie overran him, quickly reversed directions – same maneuver, same result. Each dash for freedom grew shorter and shorter until the unfortunate rabbit ended up in the salivating mouth of my dog. He killed it instantly and carried it off for a quiet dinner alone.

Only one person around Brownbranch liked to hunt rabbits: Russell Selvidge, one year younger and a year behind me in school. He hunted with a twenty-gauge shotgun and sometimes took Ol' Brownie along, the delight of my dog's life. A strange and uncomfortable feeling in my stomach came over me when I saw Russell come by Dad's store with his gun. My dog would go crazy, jumping up and down with glee, barely able to wait for Russell to buy shells for the big hunt. My first feelings of jealousy surfaced as I watched the two hunters walk across Beaver Creek bridge, Brownie running back and forth, jumping, trying to lick Russell's face as he stopped to give a much-needed petting.

Ol' Brownie loved me, I had no doubt about that, but even today it saddens me to admit that I think he loved Russell a little more. Jealousy touched me in that secret place where the green-eyed monster lurks. I never told anyone about lying in bed on dark nights thinking about Brownie when he didn't come home, knowing full well he spent the night at Russell's place and would probably be home the next morning.

Ol' Brownie loved my dad too. Of course, everyone loved Dad, especially me. I never quite understood why my dog loved Dad so much, because he seldom petted, or fed, or said anything special to him. Dad would just make a casual, friendly comment, as if he were speaking to a good friend, and Ol' Brownie would go into his jumping, twisting, turning, happy act.

One of the fondest memories of my boyhood is of one Thanksgiving afternoon when Dad said, "Leon, get Ol' Brownie and I'll get the shotgun; let's go see if we can kill us a rabbit." We lived in a big white house in Brownbranch, in four rented rooms, and the hunt took place about two hundred yards up the hill in a field grown up with bushes and tall weeds. It was one of those special Thanksgiving days with warm sunshine and mild temperatures. Oddly, we never saw a rabbit on that special day when I was totally alone with two living beings I loved so much. Brownie tried desperately to find a rabbit, sensing a once-in-a-lifetime opportunity to show Dad that he was the world's greatest rabbit dog. He seemed to know he would probably never get another chance since rabbit hunts with Dad were rare. Dad was in a good mood; I don't think he really cared whether we saw a rabbit or not. He knew how happy just the hunt would make me. There was not a rabbit in the field that Thanksgiving Day. I think, even then, I felt sorry for Brownie. He had to realize this was his chance for fifteen minutes of fame. Dad and I walked home with a warm glow of happiness, for we had been rabbit hunting with my dog.

My dad's country store, the center of commerce for our small community, was always mobbed with local farmers on Saturday when they brought produce to sell and purchased weekly supplies of groceries, feed and hardware. The adults visited, played checkers and traded stories about the past week on the farm. Some less respectable members of the community could be found behind the bluff playing poker for real money on "poker rock," a great big rock shaped like a table on the bank of Beaver Creek. The kids looked forward to Saturday too, often running wild in the delicious, unorganized free play that seems to have been lost sometime back in the fifties. We played baseball – games that sometimes led to loud arguments and even fistfights. A home run was a long hit that ended up in Caney Creek or in the gravel bar where the creek would have been if it hadn't been dried up by drought. Boys competed to see who could throw a rock the farthest while girls jumped ropes or played drop-the-handkerchief.

I remember more dogs than kids hanging around on those Saturdays; every farmer had at least two or three to help with his stock or just to keep the critters away from his chickens. Ol' Brownie once loved all the Saturday activities but started getting old, surly and less patient when little kids disturbed his afternoon nap, especially if they tried to ride him or pull his tail. One day he did the unthinkable in my dad's mind: he bit one of the kids on the arm after taking some particularly intense abuse. The child was not hurt badly, but made a big scene, crying loudly, pointing his finger at my dog, letting everyone at the store know what had happened. I wanted to say, "If you hadn't been pulling his tail, poking his eyes, and kicking him, you wouldn't have been hurt."

Dad was a caring person. He placed more value on kids than on dogs, no matter who was right or wrong. Dogs just didn't bite kids and get away with it. He was also an early-day Ozark Mountain public relations man. He recognized that people would not be likely to patronize a store that harbored a "bitin' dog." He gave Brownie a good thrashing with a big stick, in plain view of all the customers, and informed me that if it ever happened again, he would kill my dog. People who are born and make their living in the harshness of rural Missouri love their animals in a detached sort of way. After all, they are only animals, not to be grieved over as if they were human.

A few Saturdays later, my heart sank when a nine-year-old boy came screaming to his mom at the store, blood running down his cheek, the result of an encounter with Brownie. I ran over to the big white house where my dog was hiding under the porch. When I called, he came out slowly, his old head down, tail between his legs, as if to say, "I'm sorry; I did it before I could stop myself." Though a senior in high school, I had tears in my eyes and a huge lump in my throat as I held his head in my hand. He seemed to know he had made a *big* mistake. I looked up to see Dad coming from the store wearing an expression similar to Brownie's.

"Leon, go get the gun," he said quietly.

"Dad, please don't kill him. I promise I'll never let him do it again," I begged.

"I'm sorry, Son, but we don't have any choice."

I went inside for the only rifle we had ever had, a Remington single-shot twenty-two, along with two shells. Dad loaded the rifle and called Ol' Brownie, who eagerly followed, because he loved him. I've often wondered if maybe Brownie, seeing the gun, thought maybe all was forgiven and we were going rabbit hunting again. Dad walked toward the highway running between Caney and Beaver Creek bridges. Brownie was getting excited as he ran alongside. I followed behind, tears streaming down my face, begging Dad for one more reprieve.

They reached the highway. Brownie was a few yards ahead, when Dad raised the rifle to his shoulder and called my dog,

"Brownie."

The old dog stopped, turned to face Dad, and started walking back toward him, wearing one of those beautiful dog-grins on his face, tail wagging happily. My final plea smothered beneath the crack of the rifle. Ol' Brownie dropped, a bullet between his eyes, legs thrashing the gravel road a few times; then he lay still. Dad turned to me and said, "Drag him down to the creek bottom, Son." I'll never know for sure, but I think he had a tear in his eye. I know there was a break in his voice. He put a hand on my shoulder as he walked past on the way back to our house.

It wouldn't have been manly to carry a dead dog, so I took hold of his hind leg and dragged him over the road embankment toward the gravel bar. It was only a couple hundred yards, but it seemed like miles. Grief filled my heart. My final contact with Ol' Brownie, so crass, so undignified, so unloving. I dragged him through the dirt and gravel and left him lying in the shade of an old mulberry tree.

This true story is not about my dog, Ol' Brownie, but my father, who adopted me as a baby, whom I loved with all my heart. My dad was the kindest, most loving and gentle man I have ever known, but this was a lesson in principle. Sometimes you have to do things you really hate to do, even to the point of breaking your heart, but if you have to do it, you do it.

I stayed on the creek bank the rest of the afternoon, well into darkness, moving up to the bridge, leaning over the rail, tears falling into the clear, cool water below. I thought about leaving home – after all, I was seventeen – but I knew Brownie was getting old and would have gone soon anyhow, one way or the other. I also knew Dad loved my dog and me and probably hurt as much as I did, but, being a grown man, he didn't have the luxury of showing it. About bedtime, I wandered back to the big white house where Mom had kept my supper warm. Dad walked past my chair and put his hand on my shoulder again, an apologetic touch of love.

11

BROWN LAWSON

Brown Lawson walked everywhere he went, including to my dad's little country store. He lived with his seventy-five-year-old deaf sister four miles up Caney Creek. Though he was about fifty years old when I was fourteen, we became good buddies. He smiled a lot, displaying a large gold front tooth.

When farmers in the area needed a handyman, Brown usually ended up with the job, at least if it didn't require much in

Brown Lawson was everyone's friend.

the way of skill. He could milk cows, feed chickens and hogs, and handle simple tasks. He was a small man with a huge head and often bragged that he wore the largest hat of anyone he ever knew – size 8 1/2.

When the loafers tired of playing checkers, they amused themselves with Brown. He loved ice cream and could eat huge amounts; the men made bets on how much he could eat, though they had to buy it for him. He would always oblige, and using the little, flat wooden spoon provided by the ice cream company, he would eat a quart straight from a paper carton. Serious bets were placed. Could he eat another quart in fifteen minutes? Doc Boone kept the official time, because he had an Elgin pocket watch with a big second hand. When Brown was forced to take a break for a trip to the outhouse, Doc deducted that time from the fifteen minutes. Brown never failed to eat the whole second quart. Consequently, the only ones who bet against him were "new money," people who had never seen Brown in action.

Brown was a "counter." He counted everything: how many squirrels he killed, how many miles he walked, how many quarters he saved. One spring he started saving quarters, putting them into a gallon milk jar, the objective – to buy a new pump twenty-two rifle. As young boys, my friends and I liked to talk with Brown. We quizzed him about progress toward his goal. He preferred talking with us over the older men; we took him seriously.

He adhered strictly to a system in saving quarters: never changing a dollar bill into silver – that would be cheating. He only saved quarters that came his way naturally – as change – after buying something.

"How many you got now, Brown?" I asked one day when he came into the store.

"Thirty-six," he answered proudly. "Need a hundred and twenty-eight to order that Remington pump from Sears."

"What're you gonna do when you get it?"

"See how many squirrels I can kill in one season. Season starts May 31. I'm hopin' to have the gun by then. I've got thirty-six quarters now. I need a bunch more."

"How many more, Brown?" I asked, being unkind. Brown was not good at math, but his sister had looked up the twenty-two in the catalogue and told him he needed one hundred twenty-eight. He could count but wasn't good at adding and subtracting or any other kind of arithmetic. He knew if he kept saving and counting he would eventually have the required number of quarters.

"Lots," he answered, "I'm hopin' to have the gun by squirrel season."

It was the middle of May, the last day of school; kids scrambled up the hill to the store from the school-bus stop. Excitement filled the air; summer was fast approaching; no more school for months! We rushed inside, creating a commotion, heading for the pop and ice-cream cases. We noticed people were standing around something by the post office, which occupied one corner of the store.

I saw Brown standing proudly, empty milk jar in hand. On the post-office counter, Eunice Jackson, postmistress, was counting a big pile of shiny quarters, sliding those counted to one side. "Thirty-two dollars," she announced.

Brown looked at her apprehensively, then smiled when she added, "You got a hundred and twenty-eight all right." Ike Wilson saw the Sears catalog in Brown's other hand and asked to see a picture of the twenty-two. Brown quickly sat on a wooden bench, turned to the right page, and put a hairy finger on the rifle he had been dreaming about for months.

"It's a pump, ain't it?" Doc Boone asked. "That's a nice gun."

The gold tooth beamed; Brown stood happily by as Eunice filled out the Sears order blank and included a money order.

"Wonder how long it'll take?" Brown asked.

"Says here six to eight weeks," Eunice answered. "But orders usually come a lot quicker."

"Hope so," said Brown. "Squirrel season starts May 31."

Brown walked the four miles to the store every day to check the mail, often arriving before the postal service delivery truck. Two weeks passed – no gun. Three weeks, still no rifle. Squirrel season began. The men teased Brown, suggesting that maybe his money order got lost. He started sitting on the store's front porch away from them.

The gold tooth didn't show much anymore. Brown feared they had lost his order, that he would never get that beautiful twenty-two rifle. He sat alone on the porch one summer morning whittling a piece of cedar wood, when Eunice pushed the screen door partly open and said, "Brown, come 'ere."

She handed him a long box. Eyes lifted from the checkerboard; everyone in the store stopped to watch. "Must be your gun," Eunice said. "Open it."

Brown walked out on the porch, sat on the bench, and with trembling hands tried to open the cardboard box. Ike Wilson finally stepped forward with his pocketknife and helped. Brown reached into the open end, hesitated as he caressed the contents, then pulled out the rifle. The gold tooth appeared. He looked at his gun, then up at his friends.

"Good looking twenty-two, Brown," said Doc Boone. "Could I hold it?"

The proud owner handed it to his friend and beamed. All the men wanted to hold his gun, to admire the beautiful varnished finish. His gun! Never had Brown Lawson experienced such pride of ownership, such a position of admiration, and he loved it. He stood beaming, hands in overall pockets as his new twenty-two passed from one admirer to another.

"You'll have to sight it in," Ike said. "Do you know how?"

"I never done it, least not on a brand new one," Brown answered.

"Have you got any shells? I can help you if you want," Ike offered.

My dad disappeared into the store and returned with a fifty-cent box of twenty-two long-rifle shells. Long-rifle ammunition ranged farther and with more accuracy than "shorts," or little shells.

"Here, Brown, the first box is on me," Dad smiled.

The gold tooth sparkled as Brown sat on a wooden bench and inserted cartridges into the rifle's magazine. Doc Boone and Ike Wilson walked off the front porch and placed a cardboard box about twenty-five yards away. They drew a bull's-eye about three inches in diameter on the side of the box. Ike was one of the best shots around, so for the next hour he worked with Brown until the rifle's sights were lined up and demonstrated how to hit the bull's-eye twenty-five yards away.

Brown told me later he didn't sleep much that night. "I kept havin' dreams about that new rifle; I put it on the bed beside me." Sometime after midnight, he got up, lit a kerosene lamp and admired his new treasure while his sister slept in the next room. "I oiled the gun again and polished the stock, then practiced aiming at the moon outside my bedroom window."

Before sunrise, Brown was out the door with his twenty-two walking toward a big mulberry tree near Caney Creek, the best place to find squirrels at this time of year. Limbs bowed toward the ground, laden with juicy black mulberries. It was a huge old tree with a gnarled trunk at least four feet across, standing majestically on a level area about twenty feet above the small stream. Sitting with his back against the trunk, Brown felt warm and secure, probably because no one was around to tease or make fun of him. He sat silently, cross-legged, the rifle across his lap, watching gray squirrels jump from limb to limb.

The sun soon rose high enough to provide plenty of light for sighting. A little way down the hill toward the creek, a large pin oak spread huge limbs over the water, back toward the mulberry tree. Squirrels could leap from the mulberry tree and sit comfortably on one of the big oak-tree limbs to enjoy their breakfast. Brown watched as a gray squirrel sailed through the air from the mulberry to the oak, landing nimbly on a crooked limb. The squirrel found a comfortable spot, sat on its haunches holding the mulberry in its front paws, and started nibbling. Brown raised the new twenty-two and sighted in on his prey. "It would have been an easy shot," he told me, "but just when I was ready to pull the trigger, the squirrel stopped nibbling and looked right at me, almost like he was thinkin', 'Whatcha' doin'?'"

With finger on the trigger, safety off, Brown hesitated. He had killed lots of squirrels in his time, but for some reason this one was different. He lowered the barrel and watched. Squirrels barked all around him, jumping from tree to tree. He kept watching. A mother deer and baby fawn didn't see him as they stepped cautiously out of the woods on the far side of the creek and stopped for a drink. Wildflowers grew in abundance all around; their fragrance enhanced by morning dew and a soft breeze. Brown enjoyed the total silence. A large black crow, unaware of the human visitor, penetrated the silence with swishing sounds as he flew down the valley above Caney Creek.

Brown unloaded his new twenty-two and decided he could kill squirrels some other day. He closed his eyes and dreamed again, this time – he told me – about being the happiest person in the world.

12

MY BROTHER'S KEEPER

Sixteen-year-old Carl, a local boy abandoned by his father and then his mother, left to be raised by his grandparents as best they could, spent the night wherever he ended up. Fortunately, he lived in Bradleyville, a tiny Ozarks village unexposed to drugs and vices of a larger city. Carl, however, managed to find trouble even when he had to hunt for it – always fighting, skipping school, sometimes stealing what he wanted if he didn't have the money to buy it. He was a handsome boy of average size with a winning smile.

He loved to hang out at the home of the local storekeepers Max Brantley and his wife Marilyn. Max's son John was about the same age and a cousin to Carl. Marilyn felt sorry for the boy and always made him feel welcome, feeding him home-cooked meals whenever he wandered into the back part of the store building where they lived. He slept on the worn couch in their living room. He often came in and collapsed on the couch after the Brantleys were in bed. In the morning, Marilyn would rouse him at the same time as the other kids, give him a warm breakfast, and send him to school.

Other than the Brantleys and his grandparents, Carl's closest friend was his brother Joe. Joe, twenty-four, had served four years in the Marines and worked for Southern Construction, a local company that cleared right-of-ways and erected power lines for the electric co-op. Carl wanted to be like Joe.

Max Brantley took a liking to Carl and tried to talk with him about staying out of trouble and doing better in school, but it wasn't an easy task. The superintendent of schools often had to call Max to warn that Carl was just barely hanging on academically and was about to the expelled for unruliness and poor attendance.

Late one Saturday night, the Brantleys, already asleep, were awakened when Carl came staggering through the back door, making loud noises, crashing into something. Marilyn yelled for Max as soon as she saw the boy's bloody, battered face. His shirt was ripped, two front teeth were missing, his face was cut and swollen almost beyond recognition. He smelled of alcohol. After washing his face, the Brantleys loaded him in the pickup and drove to the Branson emergency room for stitches to close his facial lacerations.

"What happened?" Max asked on the way back to Bradleyville.

"Nothin'."

All attempts to get a story out of Carl failed. The family called big brother Joe.

"What happened to you?" Joe demanded of his little brother.

"Hoss," he answered quietly.

"Hoss Reed? How come?" Joe asked. "He's as old as I am. We work on the same crew. What'd he do this to you for? What'd you do?"

"Nothin'."

"Don't give me that crap. What'd you do?"

"He called me a bastard. Said I was a bastard and you was too."

"This is the last time I'm askin'. What'd *you* do that made him say that?"

"I took a screwdriver and scratched the paint on his new Dodge truck," the boy said meekly.

Joe took a big drag on his cigarette, looked at his little brother, then walked out the back door.

Marilyn put Carl to bed on the couch. It was 4 a.m. Max knew the Southern Construction crew would be gathering in the grocery store in an hour as they did every morning for coffee, lunch sandwiches and social exchanges before going off in different directions for their ten-hour day. So he dressed and walked into the dark store. A full moon shone and sent soft light inside the old building, making it easy for Max to see his way around. He didn't want to turn on lights that would attract early patrons before his regular opening time of 5:00 a.m. He checked the cooler for lunch meat and other makings for the workers' sandwiches

Max saw the red ember of a cigarette and a man on the front porch. He walked near the window and recognized Joe, standing alone, waiting. Max opened the door.

"Whatta you doin', Joe? Wanna come in?"

"No, I'm just waitin'," he answered and took another puff.

Max closed the door and sat on a counter stool. He watched as old cars and pickups slowly drove onto the lot and parked. Some sat in their rigs waiting for the store to open; others stood in small groups talking. A new bright red customized pickup with high wheels pulled onto the gravel lot. Big Hoss Reed stepped out. Max sat in the dark store watching out the front window.

Joe Dawson dropped his cigarette on the concrete porch and stepped on it. His foot lingered as he ground the cigarette out, looking at Hoss Reed. He stepped off the porch onto the parking lot and spoke in a low voice, "Hoss."

The big man turned to see who called. He glared at Joe. "Yeah?"

"Me 'n' you's got a little business to settle," Joe said as he stood in the middle of the lot, removing his jacket.

Hoss laughed. "What's your problem, Dawson? Your little brother?"

"You gotta learn not to pick on kids. You need to pick on people your own size," Joe looked straight into the big man's eyes.

"You sure as hell ain't my size, and you're liable to get the same as your little bastard brother got." Hoss peeled off a heavy woolen shirt as he walked toward Joe. "I'd advise you to tell the little bastard not to go 'round scraping the paint on people's new trucks – that's what he done."

Twenty or thirty Southern Construction workers gathered round. As Hoss got closer, Joe went into a fighting stance, fists cocked and ready. Hoss stopped a couple of steps short of Joe and stood, smiling, arms hanging at his sides. "I don't really want to have to whoop the crap outta two Dawsons the same week, but it looks like I'm gonna have to."

From inside the store, Max Brantley saw the workers form a circle around the two men as Joe charged, swinging a clinched right fist at the big man's jaw. Hoss threw up his left arm and deflected the blow, but Joe's left fist smashed his mouth, sending him backward a step.

"Now you've done it, you stupid S.O.B.!" Hoss yelled as blood poured down his chin. He charged like a bull and grabbed Joe in a bear hug with his huge hairy arms, dragging him through the bystanders, ramming his head against the fender of a truck. The circle of onlookers moved with the fighters. No one made a move to interfere. This is the way men settled things around Bradleyville.

Joe was dazed momentarily with Hoss's apelike arms crushing his chest. He freed his right arm enough to heave a tremendous backstroke, ramming his elbow into Hoss's rib cage. The hairy arms dropped as the big man coughed, trying to catch his breath, grabbing his side. Joe turned and rained lightning blows to his face and head – two hard left jabs, a right cross, two more punishing jabs. Hoss went down, but grabbed Joe's ankles and brought him down too.

Max wondered if he should go out and get the guys to break it up. Calling the law was out of the question. Bradleyville people hated the law; they settled their own problems.

Joe knew as Hoss dragged him down that he must not let the man get on top of him. Hoss outweighed him by at least seventy-five pounds and would pound his head against the rocky parking lot. He rolled over and over, but Hoss was young and agile. He crawled after and caught Joe. Joe rolled over on his back, pulled his legs to his chest and kicked Hoss in the gut with both feet, almost lifting him off the ground.

The onlookers yelled encouragement. Seldom did a day pass when they didn't see a good fight; this was just another day. Some laughed; others turned away and walked into the store when Max opened the door and flipped on the lights.

Joe sprang to his feet. Hoss was on his feet too, but he was bent over, heaving. Joe grabbed him by the head and rammed a knee into Hoss's face, again and again until the big man fell to the ground and didn't move.

The onlookers went inside the store, poured coffee and ordered lunch meat sandwiches. Joe walked back to Max's bathroom and washed the blood from his face. A couple of guys stayed with Hoss until he regained consciousness, then with one on each side to steady him, they walked him to an outside water faucet and washed off the blood.

Twenty minutes later everyone left for work.

After breakfast, Max watched as school kids began to gather in front of the store. He saw Carl walk toward Hoss's new red pickup as other boys followed. Carl took something from his pocket and made a huge scratch across the driver's side door and front fender. Max ran to the door.

"Carl! Get in here!" he yelled angrily. He grabbed the boy's arm and dragged him to the back part of the building.

"Are you crazy?" he yelled. "Don't you know Hoss Reed'll kill you?"

"Nah, my brother won't let 'im."

Max Brantley owned the country store in my hometown of Bradleyville. He told me this story about how the local people handle their own problems and how families come together when necessary. Names have been changed.

13

BOZIE'S NEW TRUCK

Ray and I watched as Bozie carefully turned the truck off the country road and drove slowly up the hill toward my parents' country store. He stopped the new blue Studebaker pickup and sat smiling, proud and happy on this Saturday evening to be at the wheel of such a fine vehicle.

"Howdy, boys," he said, continuing to sit at the wheel. "How do you like her? Pretty, ain't she?" He was talking about his dad's new Studebaker pickup that the forty-year-old had been allowed to drive on a Saturday night. "Hop in, let's go."

Ray's mom and dad had dropped him off at our house, across the road from the store, earlier that afternoon so we could ride with Bozie to Ava and go roller skating and maybe to a movie. We had not seen his new pickup.

Bozie Roberts loved to drive his dad's new Studebaker truck.

I sat in the middle, and Ray took the jump seat as we pulled onto the highway.

"Does it have a radio, Boz?" Ray asked.

"Has a cat got an ass?" Bozie said, living dangerously with such language. Smiling from ear to ear, he tuned the knob to Bill Monroe and the Bluegrass Boys. "And a heater and mud flaps and a sun visor," our forty-year-old friend added. "She's loaded. Got a big motor and fog lights."

"How fast will she go, Boz?" I asked.

"Oh, I promised Dad I wouldn't drive her fast," he said, sounding almost fearful at the thought. "He said if he heard that I was hot roddin', this'd be my last time to drive it."

It was pretty well known in our little community that Bozie was forty going on fourteen. He had dropped out of school in the fifth grade and spent his life sheltered and controlled by a domineering father. A big man, more than six feet tall, Bozie weighed at least two-hundred-fifty pounds. He wore new blue overalls with galluses hooked to shiny brass buttons and a green John Deere cap. A yellow lead pencil protruded from a red-white-and-blue plastic pencil holder in his bib pocket.

"Wonder what they're gonna say when I drive her around the square," he said, grinning again around the toothpick in his mouth. "Ain't many people that's got a new truck, much less a Studebaker."

The new truck moved smoothly over the gravel road, a chilly October breeze sweeping through open windows. Bozie kept a close eye on the speedometer, never going faster than fifty.

"Turn old Roy up," Ray said as Roy Acuff belted out "The Wabash Cannonball," coming from the Grand Ol' Opry in Nashville, Tennessee. I cranked it all the way, but Bozie turned it back down.

"Dad said to keep it low so the speakers'll last."

Bozie straightened his shoulders as we pulled into line behind the stream of old cars and pickups cruising round the Ava square.

"There's Bobby Joe," Ray announced, sticking his head out the window. "Hey, Smallwood." Louder, "Smallwood, wantta drag?"

Bobby Joe Smallwood pulled to the right side of the street slowly, as Bozie drove alongside. Ray greeted him, "How's it going? You get them new headers on your motor?"

"Yeah, that Bozie's Studebaker?" the Ava football player asked. "Does he want to try me out?"

"No," Bozie yelled. "I'm not racin' this truck." A worried look came over his face. "Told you boys I ain't drivin' this truck fast, 'specially not here in town where everbody can see. No."

Bobby Joe chuckled, "See you boys at the skating rink." He started to pull away but stopped. "You hear 'bout somebody robbin' ol' Boone's gas station and knockin' him in the head? They took Boone to the hospital. Hank's lookin' for the guy, but they ain't caught him yet." Then he raced the engine of his '50 Ford and peeled rubber as he roared around the square.

"Lordy, I hope Sheriff Hank catches whoever robbed Boone, don't you?" Bozie worried as he continued slowly around the square, passing in front of the Avalon Theater and a group of teenagers, including Glenna Ann, standing in front of the ticket booth. The words "Roy Rogers and Dale Evans" covered the small sign above the front door.

"You girls goin' skatin'?" Ray yelled. Bozie stopped.

They looked at each other, giggling. "After the show," Glenna Ann said. "You goin' to the show?"

"Let's go," I said.

Bozie pulled into an open parking space near the Avalon, and Ray and I pulled out quarters for admission. Bozie unsnapped a little leather coin purse for his quarter. Glenna and I sat together, holding hands and smiling during a pretty boring movie.

But Bozie loved it, especially the cartoon at the beginning. He sat one row in front of us, reared back in his seat, arms crossed over his chest, toothpick still clinched between his teeth, and eyes glued to the screen. He laughed heartily at the funny parts and leaned forward anxiously in the chase scenes.

As soon as the movie ended, we gathered on the sidewalk to decide what to do next.

Bozie leaned over and whispered in my ear, "Dad said I gotta have the new truck home by midnight."

"Bozie, does your old man know you're forty years old?" I asked.

"He said to be home."

"Bozie! Where's your truck?" Ray yelled. "It's gone."

The parking space was empty; the truck not there. Bozie turned pale. He was paralyzed. "Oh, Lordy. Oh, Dad'll kill me." Tears ran down his cheeks. He ran up and down the sidewalk, looking for the Studebaker, then sat on the curb, crying like a baby. I felt embarrassed for my old friend, but I also felt sorry for him. He had spent his life restricted, confined and imprisoned. Then just when he had a chance for a few hours of glory, his world fell apart. Terror gripped his heart.

"Let's go to the sheriff's office and tell Hank," I said.

"He probably ain't there," Ray said. "Out lookin' for whoever robbed Ol' Boone, but let's go see anyhow."

We hurried around to the other side of the square, and a half-block down First Street to the county sheriff's office. An old van with "Oak County Sheriff" painted on the side sat in front of the dimly lit office. Wee Willie Schrum sat in the sheriff's chair, throwing darts at a dartboard ten feet away.

"What's up, boys? Willie said in his nonchalant, high-pitched voice. He tossed another dart, completely missing the board.

"Somebody stole Bozie's dad's new Studebaker," I said.

"What!" Willie yelled as he sat up straight. "Goodness' sakes. Somebody robbed Ol' Boone's station tonight too. Hank's out huntin' for him." He looked at Bozie, who stood with hands in his overall pockets, tears running down his cheeks.

"Can't figure why anybody'd take a new Studebaker," Bozie said, his voice breaking. "My dad's gonna be awful mad."

"The guy that robbed the station was on foot, accordin' to Boone," Willie said. "Maybe he took it. Did you leave the keys in it?"

Bozie hung his head. "Yeah. We never take the keys out; no need to at home. Even Dad leaves the keys in, but I wish I had took 'em."

A royal-blue Ford screeched to a halt outside the sheriff's office. Bobby Joe Smallwood jumped out and charged into the little office. "I seen your truck, Bozie. We was drivin' back by the old cemetery when I seen it parked back in them trees, no lights or nothin', just parked there."

"Is it still there?" Wee Willie's voice pitched higher as he jumped up.

"Far's I know; it was five minutes ago," Bobby Joe said. "Let's go; I'll show you where it's at."

Bozie, Ray, and I piled into the blue Ford with Bobby Joe as Willie fumbled to strap on his gun belt.

"Are you comin'," Bobby Joe yelled. "He'll be gone before we get there."

Willie jumped in the old van. Bobby Joe started to pull out, but the van remained motionless. We waited. Nothing. "Are you comin'?" Bobby Joe yelled out the window.

"Won't start. Battery's dead. Somebody left the radio on," Willie whined.

Ray jumped out of the Ford, "For Christ's sakes, Willie. How'd you ever get this job?" He looked at Bobby Joe, "Got any jumper cables?"

"In the trunk." He opened the truck and grabbed the cables while I lifted the hood on the old van. We finally got it started, and Bobby Joe yelled at Willie, "Now foller me and don't kill it."

We pulled back onto the square and headed north toward the cemetery. The big engine in Bobby Joe's Ford roared as we raced through the small-town streets.

"Better stop, Bobby. You've plumb lost Wee Willie," Ray said.

"Man, I wish he'd hurry up," Bobby Joe stopped until the van's dim lights crept around the corner. Bobby drove slowly up the hill toward the old cemetery, turned off the lights, stopped, engine running, a half-block before reaching it. The old van started to pass when Bobby yelled, "Stop the stupid idiot." I jumped out and waved Willie to a stop.

"Don't go any farther with your lights on," Bobby Joe said. "Foller me but leave your lights off – it's light enough to see. The Studebaker was parked in that bunch of trees to the right of the graveyard."

"I ain't goin' back in them trees by the graveyard," Bozie said.

Ray looked at me, then spoke to our friend, "Whatsa matter, Boz? You scared of the graveyard?"

"I'll wait here," he said nervously. "Let Willie get my truck." He turned to Willie, "You'll get it, won't you Willie?"

Wee Willie hesitated. "Where do you reckon that guy is – he has a gun, Boone said."

"So have you got a gun?" I said. "Are you afraid, too?"

"I think that old house there next to the Studebaker is where John Baker lives, the one that everybody thinks killed his wife, but he got off," Ray said. "He's got a nephew that escaped from the pen in Oklahoma – they never caught him. I betcha he's the one that robbed Ol' Boone, and I betcha he's in that house right now with John Baker."

"Oh, Lordy," Bozie moaned, "what're we gonna do now, Willie?"

"I think we better go find Hank," Willie said, walking backward toward the old van.

"He's liable to take off," Ray whispered. "Why don't you go in there and arrest him, Willie. Me and Leon'll go with you. Pull your gun out; let's go."

The front door of the old house suddenly burst open, startling us, We sat silently in the darkness as two men walked out, one carrying a rifle, but they didn't see us.

"You've gotta get outta here, but you can't drive that damned Studebaker," John Baker said. "Why the hell did you pick the easiest rig in town to spot?"

The two men stood on the porch, silhouetted against a dim light inside the house. The second man said, "Hell, I didn't have no choice. It was the first one I seen, and the keys was in it, so I took it – didn't have time to go shoppin,'" he said, obviously agitated.

"Well, you ain't takin' my truck," Baker said, "so you can drive that damned Studebaker and be caught before you get outta town, or take off on foot."

"Gimme that gun, Willie, if you ain't gonna do nothin'," Ray whispered, reaching for the pistol. He pulled the gun from the holster and looked at me. "You goin' with me?"

"Yeah, I guess. Wish I had a gun too."

The younger man walked toward the Studebaker.

"Where you goin'?" John Baker asked.

"To get the money," the younger man said. "It's in the truck." He walked to the Studebaker, opened the door, reached inside, and withdrew a paper bag. He slammed the truck door with a loud bang, stepped back, and then kicked the shiny blue door as hard as he could, making a big dent.

A scream that sounded like an elephant shocked us as Bozie bolted toward the man who had kicked his truck. We watched his big bulky body as he flew across the yard, screaming like a wild man, racing toward the Studebaker and the man who had kicked it.

John Baker backed against the house, rifle hanging in his hand, stunned by the man raging out of the darkness. Light from a bedroom window illuminated the man by the truck, who was also startled by the sudden screams. Running backward, he yanked a gun from his coat pocket, but too late. Bozie was upon him. The big man grabbed him by the throat, lifted him off the ground, and shook him like a rag doll. The gun fell from his hand.

"You ruint Dad's truck," he said, crying like a baby. "How come you ruint my Dad's truck?" Now he was slamming the man against the side of the house, banging his head against the solid wall. He screamed again louder, as if releasing forty years of anger, and threw the limp body to the ground, kicking him over and over.

"Stop right there," John Baker said, pointing the rifle at Bozie.

"Drop that gun, John," a voice from the darkness said. "I'm aiming at your head, and I'll kill you, and I mean it." Ray Jones held Willie's cocked pistol in both hands, walking in a crouch across the dark yard. "Drop it NOW!"

Baker dropped the gun.

"Bozie, stop!" I yelled. "You're gonna kill him." I ran and grabbed the big man, trying to keep him from kicking the limp form on the ground. He was crying, but I managed to coax him over by the truck.

"Oh, Lordy, what's Dad gonna do?" he started crying again. "The door's completely bent in," he said, touching the shiny metal.

"Hank!" I heard Ray hollering. "Get over here and arrest these guys." Somehow,

Sheriff Hank heard where we were and arrived on the scene. He told John Baker to get in the sheriff's car and called the ambulance for the man Bozie had worked over.

Bozie was on his knees touching the big dent in the Studebaker's door. "What am I gonna do?" he said, looking at me.

Hank walked over. "What's the matter, Boz?"

"Look what he done to Dad's new Studebaker," he said tearfully.

Hank looked at the door. "That ain't nothin', Boz. It's just buckled in. Here, let me show you." He put his forearm against the big dent, pressed hard and fast, and let up. The dent popped back in place, good as new. "Didn't spend twenty years in the body business for nothin'," the sheriff said.

"Oh, Lordy, Hank. Thank you, Hank. Do you reckon Dad'll ever know about it?"

"Not 'less you tell him," Hank said with a smile, happy to have been of some value to someone this evening.

We left the skating rink early so Bozie could get home in time. On the way home, when we hit the two-mile-long straight stretch of road near the 4-H Club, Bozie said, "Watch this, boys." He held the steering wheel like a NASCAR driver, gradually increasing the speed. I watched the speedometer go to fifty-five, then sixty. Bozie was breathing hard, eyes glued to the road. The needle crept up to sixty-five, then seventy, as a big smile came over Bozie's face. Eyes still glued to the road, he said, "It's fun to get a little wild on Saturday night, ain't it? Don't mention this to no one."

14

TICKET TO DAYLIGHT

The worldliest people around Bradleyville in the early fifties were those who made annual trips for seasonal work in Idaho, Oregon and Washington. They came home talking about how much money they had earned picking apples, training hops, working in the wheat harvest, and other types of migrant farm work. They told about the long highway trip, emphasizing the number of car wrecks they had seen, which always fascinated the home folks.

The spring of my junior year in high school, 1952, I talked my parents into letting me go to the great Northwest in search of that easy money. Two of my buddies, Bill Blair and Russell Selvidge, made the trip with me. Bill served as our unofficial guide; he had been there before with his parents.

I am about seventeen here, the same year as my adventurous trip out west.

This time, however, no adults. We started our trip from Springfield the day after school was out and rode the bus to Kansas City, where we would depart on the westward journey aboard a Greyhound bus.

Russell and I were leaving the Ozark hills for the first time in memory. Neither of us had ever been out of the state since "growing up," except barely across the line into Arkansas to pick strawberries. Russell was a relaxed kid who smiled often and was not easily excited. Bill talked a lot, always voicing strong opinions on everything. He was a little on the "chubby" side, as our hill people would say, or a bit "stout."

I carried a small, old suitcase made of heavyweight cardboard. Mom helped me pack for the summer-long trip: an extra pair of jeans, two shirts she had made, socks, underwear and a toothbrush.

The big diesel engine whined as the bus pulled out of Springfield, heading north toward Kansas City. No teenage boys could have been more excited than the three of us. We laughed, joked and almost twisted our necks off trying to see everything. The bus made fairly regular stops to pick up passengers, for snacks and meals and to let the riders use restrooms.

The huge five-story Greyhound bus station greeted us in Kansas City, boggling our minds as we wandered around trying to see everything at once, waiting for our bus to depart. Hundreds of travelers milled around the large building, some rushing, others lounging; yet others slept on the long wooden benches. A man's voice blared over the loudspeaker, "Now departing Gate 22 for Columbia, Missouri; St. Louis; Springfield, Illinois; and Cheecaggoo. All aboard! This is the final boarding call."

We carried our tickets folded and stuffed deep in our jeans pockets. The driver from Springfield told us our bus would depart from Gate 36, going through Topeka and Salina on its way to Yakima, Washington, our final destination. He said we had about a two-hour wait and should listen for the man on the loud speaker to announce our bus.

Bill Blair was our unofficial guide since he had been out west before.

Russell pointed to a large crowd near a corner of the main lobby. We walked over to investigate and saw a large saloon. The people were looking at something inside. As we worked our way through the crowd, we finally saw the attraction – a small box sitting high above the bar with black and white moving pictures of a boxing match. A little man in front of us turned around and spoke with amazement, "That's comin' all the way from New York – it's television. Them boxers is fightin' in New York – now, right now."

Bill, Russell and I stood transfixed. We had heard about television but had never seen it. The little man continued to inform us.

Russell Selvidge liked the west so much he moved to Selah, Washington, where he still resides.

"The govermint ain't gonna let regler people have one of them in their homes. They cost about a million dollars; besides, people'd quit goin' to movie theaters." We marveled at his wisdom and watched the little black and white box until Bill had to go to the restroom.

"It's way down them long stairs," our new friend told us. "It's quite a ways. You boys better listen for your bus to be announced over the loudspeaker. You wouldn't want to miss your bus. And be careful who you talk to; they's some bad apples around here."

We hurried down the long stairs to the largest restroom we had ever seen. Back home, we didn't even have restrooms. We used outhouses. There must have been fifty stalls, all private. Bill tried to go in one, but the door was locked.

"Well, I'll be damned," he yelled. "Would you look at this."

Russell and I walked over to see what he was pointing at. It read, "Insert nickel and turn knob."

"You gotta pay a nickel to take a crap," Bill was amazed, but in no condition to delay, so he put the nickel in and shoved the door open. Russell and I waited, and waited, and waited.

"Whatta you doin' in there?" I yelled. "You're gonna make us miss the bus!" At that instant, a voice came on the loudspeaker.

"Now boarding out of Gate 36 for Yakima, Washington, with stops at Toopeeka, Saalina, Haays, Kansas; and Denver, Colooooraadoo. All aboard!"

Russell yelled, "Bill! Our bus's leavin'! Come on! Hurry up!"

I heard Bill moan from behind the toilet door as the toilet paper roller hummed.

"Bill, we're gonna run on up there!" I yelled.

"NO!" he screamed. "Don't leave me! Wait!" He started trying to open the door. Slam! Slam! Slam! In a frenzied state, he kept trying to force the door outward when it was designed to open inward. Wham! Bang! "This damned door's stuck! I can't get out!" he yelled frantically.

Other people began to gather round, and I kept hollering, "Open it the other way." The slamming continued, increasing in intensity. "Don't let that damned bus leave me!" He was almost crying. The slamming stopped, and the next thing I saw was his head on the floor squeezing through the small opening between the bottom of the door and the not-too-clean restroom floor. He had to struggle hard to get his "chubby" body through the opening.

A tall skinny cowboy bent over laughing as Bill jumped up and tried to wipe off the front of his shirt. "Let's get the hell outta here," he said.

Our big bus whined out of the Kansas City station about midnight. Despite the exciting day, I fell into a deep sleep right away, my head against the window. A few hours later I opened my eyes and sat transfixed; I saw nothing but flat land as far as I could see in the early-morning light. We could have been on the ocean, but instead of waves of water and foam, waves of wheat swayed in the breeze. Out the back window, I saw a spectacular sunrise wash over the golden fields of wheat. I sat up and shook Russell.

"Look," I whispered. "Ain't that somethin'? You ever see anything like that?"

Russell kicked Bill, "Wake up. Ain't' no trees! Where are we?"

"Must be Kansas," I whispered.

The road was straight, level and seemingly endless. The bus hummed along like a big ship cruising an ocean of wheat. Most passengers dozed or slept soundly, heads hanging at odd angles. A big fat man across the aisle, sitting next to a woman with a baby, chain-smoked. Two seats in front of him a little shrunken man with a long beard nipped at a bottle of whiskey taken from his hip pocket. Finally, the driver slowed as we entered a small town and pulled into a bus station.

"Salina, Kansas, folks. We've got a thirty-minute rest stop. Restrooms and restaurant inside."

The sweetness of fresh morning air greeted us as we stepped off the bus and headed straight for the café. Eggs over easy with bacon and coffee laced with lots of sugar and cream tasted great. Not wanting to miss the bus, we ate hurriedly before going to the restroom. There we were intrigued with all sorts of interesting things scribbled on the wall, which we had never seen at home. Feeling it was our duty to leave our mark, we wrote our names, addresses, and the date.

A voice came over the loudspeaker. "Ladies and gentlemen, we have an announcement to make. All passengers please come to the restaurant."

We hurried back and stood outside the restaurant door. A man wearing a suit and tie stood to one side of the room waiting for everyone to settle down, then he said, "Folks, I've got some bad news. The drivers for Greyhound Bus Lines have gone on strike as of this hour. The Greyhound bus you arrived on will not be moved now. However, as a representative of the Greyhound Company, I've been authorized to assure you that your ticket will be honored, and one way or another, Greyhound will get you to your destination."

That didn't bother us. We were in no hurry, so we went back to the restroom and finished writing on the walls and read some of the more clever poems. Bill was careful not to get locked in the stall. We spent the next two hours playing pinball machines in the station.

IS THIS THE BUS TO DENVER?

The loudspeaker came on. "Ladies and gentlemen, those of you bound for Denver and points beyond are instructed to board the Trailways bus at Gate number 8. Your luggage will be loaded on that bus."

Everyone rushed to Gate 8; we ended up near the end of the line. I looked around as someone tapped my shoulder.

"Is this the bus to Denver?" she asked. I was somewhat startled to see a beautiful brown-haired young woman standing behind me. Her sky-blue eyes and snow-white teeth rendered me nearly speechless, but I managed to respond.

"Yeah, that's where we're goin'. Then we're gonna go on to Yakima, Washington."

She nearly paralyzed me with the most stunning smile I'd ever seen. After a hearty, lyrical laugh, she said, "Well, looks like neither one of us is going to get on this bus. Lots of people ahead of us." She must have been twenty or twenty-one. Her long hair curled over her frilly white blouse, reaching almost to her tiny waist. She was tall, almost as tall as I was, and slender. Her pedal-pusher pants fit tight, reaching mid-calf on her shapely leg.

Bill and Russell turned around.

"These your friends?" she asked.

"Yeah, Bill and Russell," I answered.

"My name's Jeanne." She shook each of our hands. Her hand was soft with long, slender fingers. Her firm grip felt good, especially as she continued to smile and laugh.

We finally crowded on the bus, only to find all seats taken except the one in the very back, running all the way across the width of the bus. Only an old lady with a big straw hat sat on the left side of the back seat. Bill sat on the right side as far from her as possible. I sat next to him, Jeanne plopped down on my left, and Russell sat between her and the old lady.

The driver stood and addressed the passengers. "It's going to be warmin' up in here so you can lower the windows if you want to. Use the ashtrays and don't stomp out cigarettes in the aisle. We should be in Denver by midnight, but we'll be stopping a few times between here and there."

I continued to be fascinated by the flat land and millions of acres of wheat. Great fields of bright yellow sunflowers also waved in the wind. The aroma of Jeanne's perfume wafted over us. She kept wiggling, trying to get comfortable. Finally, even though it was mid-afternoon, she went to sleep, her head gradually sliding over to rest on my shoulder. I didn't want to move. Bill leaned forward, looked at her head on my shoulder and then whispered in my ear.

"That's the best damned lookin' woman I ever seen, don't you think?"

I nodded.

"Where's she goin'?" he continued to whisper.

I answered by shaking my head slowly, trying to tell Bill I didn't know.

The old lady reached across Russell and took Jeanne's arm, "Young lady, straighten up. Stop botherin' these boys."

Jeanne sat up and looked at the old woman. She said nothing for a moment, then she spoke, "Look, you keep your damned hand off me, old woman, if you don't want it broke, and mind your own business." Her voice was strong as she looked the woman right in the eye. "Don't you touch me again."

The old lady didn't respond. She leaned back and looked straight ahead.

Bill, Russell and I tensed, half expecting a fight to break out any second, but Jeanne grabbed me by the arm and laughed. "I didn't bother you, did I, Honey?"

"No, you didn't bother me one bit. You can do it again if you want to, if you're sleepy, I mean, just go right ahead, do it again." I glanced at the old lady who gave me a cold stare then looked away.

"You're such a sweetie," Jeanne said, then planted a big kiss on my cheek. I thought I was going to faint. Bill and Russell stared, open-mouthed. Jeanne laughed again. "Let's do something. How about cards? You boys know how to play cards?"

Bill piped up, "I can play poker an' I got a deck o' cards."

"We all know how to play poker," Russell announced. "We do it all the time at home, mostly penny ante."

"Well, bring out the cards, Handsome," Jeanne said to Bill. "Let's draw high card to see who deals first."

Bill's hands shook, and he dropped the cards. He quickly dropped to his knees and retrieved them. Jeanne laughed. "Okay, let's draw for high card." She took a card after Bill fanned the deck, laying them face down on the small space between Jeanne and me. We each took one.

I drew an eight, Russell a ten. Bill smiled as he held up a king.

"Not good enough, Handsome," Jeanne said, holding the ace of hearts. "I'll deal." She shuffled cards like a pro, fanning, cutting, slicing, and held the deck out for me to cut.

Then, flashing the perpetual smile, she said, "Since we don't have no table, I'll just put each one's card in his lap." We agreed. "Ever'one ante up a penny," she added.

She turned to her left, took the top card and placed it firmly in Russell's lap, and then her hand lingered as she pressed it down. She watched and laughed aloud as his face turned red. He sat stiffly as she looked him in the eye. She did the same to Bill, then me, rendering both of us nearly speechless. She gave an extra downward push on Bill's lap and howled with laughter when he swallowed his gum.

The old lady spoke, "Young lady, I'm going to report you to the driver. You're botherin' these boys and it ain't right."

Jeanne turned on her like a tiger. "Why don't you shut up! Mind your own business, you crabby old bitch. If I want your advice, I'll ask for it. Leave us alone." Then she turned back to the game with her usual smile.

The game proceeded until we reached Hays, Kansas, and Jeanne had won most of our change before the driver announced a rest stop.

"Well, I can see you boys just ain't up for the game," she said. "Can't understand why y'all seem so distracted." She laughed again as she turned to Russell, put her arms around him, pulled him close, and gave him a big squeeze, kissing him on the lips. She did the same with Bill and me before she hopped up and twisted down the aisle for the rest stop. We sat stunned. The old lady looked at us and grunted as she got up and waddled off the bus.

The Trailways bus took us on to Denver, another huge city with another beehive bus station. We changed buses around 2 a.m., heading for Salt Lake City, over the Rocky Mountains. A bright moon lit the Rockies, an awesome sight to three teenagers from the Ozark hills. Jeanne showed us how to "unpop" our ears by holding our noses and blowing. The bus made regular stops at small towns, letting some passengers off, others on. Each time, the driver woke dozing passengers by going to the outside of the bus, opening the luggage compartment, and slamming luggage in and out. A large dark-skinned man waited while the driver retrieved a coop of baby chicks from the luggage compartment. We admired the uniformed driver, thinking there were probably very few people who could qualify for such a great job.

Salt Lake City, Utah. Mormons. Men with several wives. I had read about Brigham Young bringing his people to Utah and how the Lord sent seagulls to eat the locusts devastating their crops.

The driver pulled into the station, stopped, then stood looking at his passengers.

"Folks, I don't know where you're going from here, but some of you may have to go by train. Trailways don't go everywhere that Greyhound does, so some of you that bought Greyhound tickets may have to take a train. You'll have to get in line at the ticket counter and ask the agent."

Jeanne walked to the head of the line and asked the agent what we were supposed to do. She was going to Yakima too. We hung back, watching, as the fat agent, wearing granny glasses, pointed out something to our new friend. She smiled and came prancing back.

"They's a Trailways bus over here that'll take us across town to the train depot. Let's go." Thirty minutes later the bus dropped us off at the train station.

The train conductor examined our Greyhound tickets, then directed us to a passenger car. The large comfortable seats surprised us. Russell and I sat on one side of the aisle, Bill and Jeanne across from us. All sorts of people filed onto the train – Indians; Mexicans; real cowboys with hats, boots and spurs; soldiers; sailors; and Marines. A young Mexican woman frowned as she dragged a child in each hand, looking over her shoulder at two or three other kids following her. Two loud-talking soldiers sat behind Bill and Jeanne. One of them leaned over the seat, looking at Jeanne.

"Hey, honey, how 'bout comin' back here and settin' on my lap? Whatta you say? Who's that with you, your baby brother?" He laughed.

As the grinning soldier leaned over Jeanne's seat, Bill drove a fist square onto his mouth. The straight blow knocked him backward. Bill jumped over the seat, pummeling the soldier, but his buddy started beating on Bill's back. I jumped the second soldier, got him in a hammerlock, and dragged him onto the aisle floor, slamming his head against a seat.

Jeanne was standing in her seat screaming, "Kill the bastards!"

The conductor stopped the fight and made the soldiers move to another rail car, warning Bill and me, "Any more trouble and you'll be off the train." I looked at a big knot on Bill's jaw; he pointed out that my nose was bleeding.

"You guys showed 'em," Jeanne said, grinning broadly.

We slept in our seats that night, waking at sunrise as the train labored up a mountain, pulling cars I could see winding behind us, far down in the valley. Huge snow-covered mountains reaching into the clouds and beyond awed me.

We were hungry. Jeanne told us about the dining car where we could get all kinds of good things to eat. We followed her, walking through one car after another, passing sleeping passengers, until we reached what looked like a small café. It was like nothing we had ever seen – fancy tablecloths, shiny silverware and waiters dressed in tuxedos.

I ordered two eggs over easy with bacon. The eggs seemed small to me, and only three little pieces of bacon. Then came the bill – a dollar and a quarter! I couldn't believe it! A dollar and a quarter for two little eggs and three little strips of bacon. I asked the waiter if it was a mistake. He smiled and said it was correct. Bill and Russell were equally shocked. We decided not to eat another bite in that place.

The train stopped at almost every little town, taking on and letting off passengers, delivering and receiving mail and other cargo. At Pocatello, Idaho, we discovered the train would delay about thirty minutes, so Jeanne, with the three of us, charged off the car and ran down the street to a little grocery store. We pooled our money and bought two pounds of bologna, two loaves of white bread, a small jar of mustard, and half a dozen bottles of pop. Back on the train we enjoyed the sandwiches even more after calculating how much we had saved by avoiding the dining car.

The train chugged its way north through Idaho Falls into Montana. Every minute was exciting to us – the huge mountains, strange people, but especially Jeanne. As we approached Butte, Montana, the conductor stopped by our seats, asking to see our tickets.

"You're going to have to get off at Butte this evening," he said. "This train doesn't go to Yakima. The next train toward Yakima doesn't leave until eight o'clock tomorrow morning."

"Where we s'posed to spend the night?" Bill asked.

"They's hotels in Butte – cheap," the conductor said.

We were a little apprehensive about spending the night in a strange town but got off the train, luggage in hand. Russell suggested we sleep in the train station, but Bill and I wanted to check out the town to see how much a hotel room cost. The streets were filled with pickup trucks and men on horseback, wearing big ten-gallon hats, boots and spurs. A bearded old miner threw the reins of his burdened donkey over a hitching rail in front of a rickety clapboard house. The train conductor had told us that Butte was built atop a huge hole in the ground where miners had dug for copper. I thought the old guy with the donkey must not have been one of the lucky ones.

We felt as if we were living in the Old West as we walked down the board sidewalk. The buildings were old, made of wood, mostly unpainted. I noticed cowboys looking in our direction and couldn't understand until I saw Jeanne casting her bright smile toward them. She wore tight jeans and a bright red, sheer blouse.

Russell looked at her and said, "Where you gonna spend the night?"

"Same place as you," she answered, surprised he would ask.

Bill and I looked at each other. He smiled.

Stores and shops lined the crowded board sidewalk. Horses tied to hitching rails snorted, stomping and swishing flies with their tails. A tall cowboy walked out of a saloon with a heavyset, dark-haired girl on his arm and a pistol holstered at his side, spurs jangling. They both laughed loudly at something that must have happened inside, then piled into an old Ford pickup, taking off in a cloud of dust.

"Let's go in and get somethin' to drink," I suggested.

"They won't let you drink in there," Russell said. "You gotta be twenty to drink in a bar or saloon."

"Won't hurt to try," Jeanne said.

It took a minute or so for our eyes to adjust to the darkness. I saw more cowboys, some playing pool, others sitting at the bar. Tex Ritter sang "Blood on the Saddle" from the old jukebox in the corner. A long bar ran down the left side of the large room; booths lined the other wall; tables filled the space between; and a small dance floor covered with sawdust lay in front of an empty bandstand.

"Let's get outta here," Russell said.

"I wanna drink first," I said, as I took a stool at the bar. My friends took stools on my left, and a lean cowboy sat to my right. He gave me a surly look, leaning forward to look down the bar at Jeanne. He was missing several teeth and wore a week-old, dirty beard. My heart beat fast as the big mustached bartender walked toward me.

"Yeah?" he barked.

I saw a Budweiser poster behind the bar. "Gimme a Bud," I said as confidently as I could.

He looked at Russell sitting to my left.

"Nothin', I don't want nothin'," he said hurriedly.

"Give me and the girl a Bud, too," Bill said quickly.

The bartender placed the beers before us and said, "Seventy-five cents."

Jeanne, Bill and I each put a quarter on the bar. Bill grabbed the glass of foamy beer and took a big drink. Jeanne did the same. I had never tasted beer but thought this was the time to go for it, turning the glass up and taking three big gulps. It tasted horrible. I made a face and set the glass on the bar.

The cowboy stood and walked down by Jeanne. "Come on, Honey. Me 'n' you's gonna dance."

"No, thanks, Mister," she answered.

He grabbed her arm and yanked her off the stool. "I said we's gonna dance! Come on!"

Bill started to help Jeanne, but the cowboy punched him full in the face, sending him backward to the floor, blood gushing from his nose. I jumped the cowboy, swung him around with my left hand and felt his remaining teeth crunch when my right fist smashed into his mouth. Bill recovered, and we both jumped on him, pounding the back of his head, or wherever we could get a lick in. Russell held the screaming Jeanne as she tried to kick the downed cowboy.

The big bartender grabbed us, a massive arm around each of our necks. "Get the hell outta here – you too, lady – right now before I have your asses throwed in jail."

Jeanne wiped blood from Bill's bleeding nose as we walked down the sidewalk. A wooden sign reading, "Hotel. Cheap Rooms," extended from an old four-story building. We walked inside and saw an old woman sitting behind the front desk reading a newspaper. She looked at us over wire-rimmed spectacles, eyes lingering on Jeanne's low-cut blouse and tight pants.

"This ain't no red-light district," she said. "Young lady, you'll have to get a separate room."

"She's our sister," I said without thinking. They all looked at me, surprised. "We need your cheapest room with two double beds. How much'll that be?"

The old woman frowned but apparently decided she didn't want to take a chance on losing a customer. "Four dollars for one night on the fourth floor. They's a bathroom down the hall, only one to a floor. Pay me now."

We each handed her a dollar. She gave me a long skeleton key.

"Room four-fifteen. Rowdiness and getting too loud'll get you throwed out. And you won't get your money back either," she warned.

Moldy-smelling, rickety stairs led up four flights to the top floor, where we met an old man walking down the narrow hallway, holding a walking cane in one hand, a cigarette in the other. He coughed and hacked but never bothered to look at us as we passed.

"Here it is, four-fifteen," Russell said.

Two double beds took up almost all the space in the small room. No chair, no lamp, just a single light bulb hanging from the ceiling. Beside the window lay a coiled rope, one end secured to the wall with a big spike. A hand-scribbled sign resting on the cord said, "In case of fire, throw rope out window and climb down." I laughed at the thought of the old man in the hallway climbing four stories down the rope.

The window was open; we could hear street sounds and noise from the saloon. It was close to midnight, and I was ready for bed. We looked at one other, not knowing quite what to do next. Jeanne laughed and started unbuttoning her red blouse. "You boys can stand around all night if you want, but I'm goin' to bed." She soon had nothing on but her bra and pedal pushers. After hanging her blouse on a wall hook, she reached into the little black bag with all her belongings. She pulled out a huge T-shirt and threw it on the bed, then unzipped her pants.

Russell spoke quickly, "I'll turn off the light."

"No!" she yelled. "I ain't ashamed of nothin'." She shoved her pants to the floor, revealing red bikini panties, and slid the T-shirt over her head. It came almost to her knees.

Bill, Russell and I stood transfixed as she reached under the T-shirt, obviously unhooking her bra.

"Tadaaa!" she yelled, then laughed and whirled the red bra around her head, then hung it on the same wall hook as the blouse, and jumped in the middle of one of the old beds. She scooted under the covers and looked at us, still laughing.

"Who's gonna sleep with me? Ain't room for three of you in that one little bed."

Bill and I yelled at the same time, "I am!"

"Nope," Jeanne said. "I want him to sleep with me," pointing to Russell. "Come on, Sweetie."

"No, I ain't a doin' it," he said, nervous and agitated. "I'll sleep on the floor."

Eventually, everyone bedded down, with Russell on a quilt by the door. I flipped the light out. It must have been about three in the morning when I heard Jeanne scream, Bill holler, and a thump on the floor. I jumped up and turned on the light as Bill was getting up off the floor from between the beds. Jeanne was laughing.

"Damn," Bill complained. "You didn't have to kick me plum off the bed." He rubbed his backside and crawled back in bed with me.

"Told you I didn't want to sleep with you, Buddy Boy," Jeanne said, smiling broadly.

The next morning we bought more bologna and light bread before boarding the train. The Montana plains soon turned to mountains as the one-hundred-car train wound around and between the peaks. Bill wouldn't sit by Jeanne because he was mad, and Russell wouldn't sit with her because she embarrassed him. Jeanne sat with me.

"You gotta girlfriend?" she asked, smiling as usual.

"Sorta," I answered, "but not really."

"You ever fool around with her?" She couldn't mind her own business.

"No," I said quickly.

"Not even a little bit, like kissin' and huggin' and maybe feelin' a little?" She wouldn't shut up. "You probably need somebody to show you how, don't you?"

"No."

"I could show you." She scooted closer as Bill and Russell watched.

"Get back," I said, moving closer to the window, removing her hand from my thigh. She threw her head back and let out one of those beautiful ringing laughs. People looked in our direction.

"You can put your hand on *my* leg," Bill said from across the aisle. He was over his mad spell.

"No, I want him," she said, pointing at Russell. He turned away quickly and looked out the window. "Hey, Sweetie," she purred to our buddy. "Can I come over and set on your lap?"

Russell continued looking out the window, pretending not to hear.

"You can set on mine," Bill said.

"Nope. Trade seats with me," she said to Bill. They quickly switched. Jeanne leaned over and tapped Russell on the shoulder. "Honey, I'm sleepy. Can I lay my head in your lap?" Without waiting for an answer, she put her pretty head right in his lap, brown hair covering his lap and legs.

Russell froze. He looked down at her, then quickly back out the window.

"Whewee!" Bill yelled. "Boy, you gotcha a lapful there, Russell, ol' boy." He laughed and stared hungrily as Jeanne pretended to get comfortable, wiggling her head, burrowing deeper into Russell's rigid form.

"Your lap ain't a very good pillow," she said, looking up at him. "You got something hard in your pocket?"

"No," he answered, trying to get up, but she pushed him back into the seat.

"Hold still!" Jeanne scolded. "I didn't get no nap yet."

"Wheweee!" Bill said. "Let me set there, Russell." His voice sounded a little desperate.

The train conductor, a black man wearing an official blue uniform with brass buttons and stripes, walked down the aisle collecting tickets. He stopped and looked at Jeanne.

"Young lady, sit up and leave that boy alone, else I'll move you to another car. Tickets, please." Jeanne reluctantly sat up, rolling her eyes, to the great relief of our friend Russell. We scratched around until we found our tickets and gave them to the conductor.

Early next morning the train pulled into Yakima, Washington. We got off and watched as a big fat man twice as old as Jeanne, wearing a blue suit, vest, necktie and cowboy hat, threw both arms around our girl companion, gave her a big kiss on the lips, and walked away with her. She looked over her shoulder and flashed that heartbreaking smile as she waved goodbye.

"He ain't her dad," Bill observed.

A DATE WITH DONNA

We found no work in Yakima but hired on at a cold-storage plant for peas in nearby Milton-Freewater, Oregon. We worked the twelve-hour night shift and slept during the day in a cheap basement room with three cots, spending most of our waking hours arguing about who had the hardest job. One morning, after twelve long hours of work, Bill and I almost came to blows, each angrily insisting that the other's job was easy in comparison to his own.

That job ended after a few weeks. Bill's parents joined us, and Bill and Russell went with them back to Yakima. I heard about a good job working the wheat harvest in the Horseshoe Mountains near Walla Walla, Washington. I needed a way to get around, so I spent some of my hard-earned money and bought a 1938 Chevy for $69 and drove north of Walla Walla, home of the Washington state penitentiary. A winding dirt road led from the highway, then several miles into the mountains and to the Rea Ranch.

Big John Rea hired me to tend header on a large combine machine. Wheat grew on mountains so high and steep that I couldn't believe machinery would negotiate the inclines. A huge Caterpillar tractor pulled the combine, and massive log chains running from the dozer kept it from tumbling down the mile-long mountainside. My job as a header tender involved handling a wheel that controlled the height of wheat-cutting blades. We workers lived in a bunkhouse; ate breakfast, lunch, and dinner at the ranch house; and made fifteen dollars a day, plus room and board: a very good job in those days.

A special bonus for me was Donna, the beautiful sixteen-year-old daughter of ranch foreman Cody Wellington. Cody was a massive man with arms so hairy you could barely see any skin. He never smiled.

Shortly after beginning the job, I was promoted to truck driver, hauling combined wheat from the fields to elevators near the ranch house. That route passed Cody's house, where Donna spent most of the day sunbathing in their front yard. We soon became friendly. She was tall and long-legged, well put together, and looked a couple of years older than her sixteen years. Green eyes lit up her beautiful face. She had flawless brown skin and white teeth. Donna was home alone most days since her mother worked as one of the ranch house cooks a mile away.

One afternoon I honked as my truck roared past her front yard, then did a double-take as I passed the house. She was wearing a tiny yellow polka-dot bikini, which I knew she had managed to get without her mother's knowledge. She waved and smiled. I hurried on to the elevator, unloaded in record time and headed back to her front yard. Knowing other trucks would be coming by soon, I ran to the front gate where she greeted me with a big kiss. She stepped back and struck a sexy pose, turning to give me the best view of her in her new bikini.

"Wanna go to a show tonight?" I asked breathlessly, hearing a truck lumbering down the mountain.

"Sure," she said. "What time?"

"I'll pick you up at 8:30," I said and ran back to my truck.

After the workday ended, I showered, dressed, and headed for the Wellington residence.

She was waiting on the front porch and charged across the yard as I drove up. Cody stood at the front door glaring at me. Donna jumped into the old Chevy, sitting properly on her side until we drove out of sight, then scooted so close I could hardly get to the floorboard gearshift. She threw her arms around me and started kissing my cheek, my ear, my chin, all over my face and neck.

"You're gonna make us have a wreck," I said, without too much conviction.

"Just drive slower, or stop," she said. "No one goes on this road after dark anyhow." The narrow dirt road wound in hairpin turns, switching back precariously down the steep mountain, a solid wall of dirt on one side and a precipitous drop of hundreds of feet only a few inches away on the other. I stopped the old car, turned off the lights and set the emergency brake.

Our young passion flared. We kissed and touched and caressed. Visions of Donna in that bikini burned in my mind. She unbuttoned my shirt as I did the same to her pretty white blouse. Just as we were both completely undressed and in the back seat, she yelled.

"Oh, my God! Here comes a car! My dad, I bet."

I thought I would have a heart attack. I looked up and saw headlights, still at least a mile away but coming fast down the winding road. Hairy-arms Cody Wellington would kill me. I started to put on my jeans, but she screamed, "Drive, hurry!"

I dropped my jeans and jumped into the driver's seat. At first, the old car wouldn't start, but finally it did. I rammed it into low gear and roared down the hill, leaving a huge cloud of dust behind.

"Go faster! He's gainin'!" she yelled, yanking on her pants and quickly fastening her bra. "Hurry! Hurry!"

My knees knocked with fear, not from the perilous turns and defying death every few feet, but from the thought of facing Cody Wellington as I sat naked in the car with his baby daughter. Donna screamed as I roared out of a U-turn, right rear wheel off the road, the old car balancing for a split-second between life and death.

"You hurry up!" I yelled. "Get your clothes on and take the wheel so I can get mine on!"

"Oh, God, he's almost caught us," she cried as she jumped into the front seat, blouse on, but still unbuttoned.

"Here, take the wheel!" I jumped into the back seat to get my clothes as Donna slid under the steering wheel, still buttoning her blouse. The oncoming car, now only a hundred yards behind us, obviously had difficulty with the cloud of dust. I felt my car surge even faster as I grabbed my britches. She was pouring it on. The radio had a short in it – it was either off or blasting at top volume. The song it was trying to play was Hank Williams' "Your Cheatin' Heart."

"Be careful!" I hollered. "You're gonna kill us!"

"No, Daddy is! Oh God, he's gainin'!" She was crying, but drove with a vengeance, flooring the foot feed, sliding around perilous curves that would have scared us to death if it had been daylight. I never got dressed so fast in my life and jumped back into the front seat.

"Scoot over, let me drive!" I yelled as we changed places again on the fly. I could see the gas station at the bottom of the hill where our dirt road hit the highway, now only a half-mile away. Despite our driving at breakneck speed down the narrow mountain road, the other car was right on my rear bumper, only feet, maybe even inches, away, horn blaring.

Donna scrunched against the passenger door, now fully clothed, even her anklets and shoes. I was still barefoot. "Tell him the car died and wouldn't start, but then it did," she said, biting her lip, looking back at the tailgater.

No use trying to get away now, I thought, and pulled into the old gas station with the other car still riding my rear bumper. He was blinking his lights, signaling me to stop. I stopped. Donna sat, frozen, staring straight ahead, waiting for hell's wrath. My teeth chattered, and the underarms of the shirt I had just put on were soaked.

The driver of the car behind left its lights on. He sounded the horn, a long, loud blast, rattling our nerves even more. We sat still, waiting, then heard doors open.

"Hey, boy!" a loud voice boomed. "How come you was parked up there?"

It wasn't Cody Wellington's voice. I looked around. There stood Neil, Bobby and Vince, three of my co-workers in the wheat harvest. They bent over laughing as they walked up to the windows of my car. Donna rolled up her window, refusing to look at them. I jumped out and charged Neil, slamming him to the ground. He continued to laugh uncontrollably. The others pulled me off.

"You crazy bastard!" I yelled. "You almost killed us!"

They rolled with laughter. Vince pointed to my bare feet. "You leave home barefooted?" They continued to enjoy themselves as I got back in the car and drove down the road. Donna was silent.

"Where's a good place to park?" I asked meekly.

"Take me home right now," she answered, scooting even closer to the door, putting as much distance as possible between us.

POKER & THE LUCKY SALOON

Wheat harvest ended, and I had saved $550 for spending money during my senior year at Bradleyville High School. The work hands went their separate ways, and I ended up at the Greyhound bus station in Walla Walla on a Saturday night. The ticket office was closed, so I put my old suitcase in one of the lockers and decided to check out the town. It reminded me of Butte, Montana, saloons every few doors, board sidewalks and real cowboys riding horses down Main Street.

A neon sign above the board sidewalk blinked, "Lucky's Saloon." I walked in to see if I they would serve me a beer. The bar stools were saddles; I straddled one, put my feet in the stirrups and ordered a beer. No problem. The bartender put the cold glass in front of me without a second look.

Pretty cool, I thought, feeling completely grown-up. A couple of stools away sat a kind-looking middle-aged man wearing the ever-present western hat and boots. He smiled and asked where I was from. I told him Missouri, and I was heading home on a Greyhound bus after saving $550 from wheat harvest. We made small talk until he got up and started toward the back of the room. He stopped and turned.

"You don't like to play poker, do you?"

"Yeah, I really do. We played at the bunkhouse all the time."

"Well, the boys is havin' a little game here in the back room tonight. You can join us if you want."

I grabbed my beer and followed him through some curtains into a back storeroom behind the bar. Four men sat around a table with a single one-hundred-watt bulb hanging above. The dealer wore sunglasses and a visor cap. A cigarette hung from his lips. The others wore cowboy hats. A fifth of black label Jack Daniels sat in the middle of the table.

"Shorty, this here boy's waitin' for a bus. He knows how to play poker and would like to set in for a few hands," my new friend announced.

Shorty adjusted the visor and nodded toward an empty chair.

"Set," he said, shuffling the cards. "Help yourself to a drink if you want to."

My friend sat beside me as Shorty dealt the cards. The men around the table drank straight from the bottle. Everybody smoked. A blue haze drifted above the table.

I pulled out my billfold, opened the secret compartment where I kept five one-hundred-dollar bills, took all the money out and placed it next to my cards. I still had a fifty-dollar bill in my shoe.

"Here, I'll give you chips for your money; let me have it," Shorty said.

I was a little taken aback but pushed the five hundred dollars across the table. He counted out five hundred dollars worth of chips. "Now, help yourself to the bottle, Boy. Don't be bashful."

I was playing real poker with real men in a real old-west saloon. I took a big swig of Jack Daniels and struggled to hide near-strangulation. A warm glow immediately rushed through my body; three aces in my hand of five-card draw increased that warm glow. Wonder what Bill and Russell would think if they could see me now, I thought. I took another swig of Jack Daniels.

The dealer dealt me two cards, a pair of deuces. I had a full house on the first hand. I played it cool but couldn't help but bet the maximum the first time around and raised the next time, winning fifty dollars on the very first hand. I took another stimulating swig of Jack Daniels; this one went down real smooth. What will they think back home if I get there with a thousand dollars, or even two thousand? I could buy a brand new V-8 Ford for less than two thousand. It would be pretty nice to drive a new Ford my senior year in high school.

A few hours later I left the Lucky Saloon with only the fifty dollars in my shoe, like my old friend taught me years before. I accidentally turned over my chair getting up from the table and stumbled. Shorty helped me out the door.

"Bus station's the other direction, 'bout two blocks that way," Shorty pointed.

I managed to retrieve my suitcase and get to the edge of town, where I started hitchhiking at two o'clock in the morning. A big Mack truck pulling a logging trailer stopped; I climbed into the cab.

"Where you headed, Pardner?" the driver asked. He was a little skinny guy with a goatee.

"I don't care – wherever you are, I guess." I leaned back and went to sleep. Next thing I knew he was shaking my shoulder.

"Hey, Boy, this is as far as I go. Get out."

It was still dark in the middle of downtown Pendleton, Oregon. I staggered down the street carrying the old suitcase until a police car pulled alongside. The officer said, "You got a problem, Buddy? Where you goin'?"

"I don't know," I said honestly. "Nowhere, I guess."

"I could put you in jail for vagrancy, you know," he said not too convincingly.

"Fine. That's fine with me," I said. "I need a place to sleep."

"Get in the car," the cop ordered.

I got in the front seat, suitcase on my lap. "You gonna put me in jail?"

"No, I'm takin' you out to the edge of town where you can get a ride." He was an older man who seemed genuinely concerned. "Now, be careful," he said as I got out of the police car.

Another logging truck picked me up, and I promptly fell asleep again. Sometime later I felt a hand shaking my shoulder. "I turn off here, Son."

I climbed down from the big truck and stood beside the mountain road as he turned up a narrow logging trail. As soon as the grinding of the truck's gears and the diesel engine died away, perfect quiet reigned. Tall pines stretched majestically through the early morning fog, trying to rise above it. Golden sun rays streamed between trees, the beginning of another late-August day. A large buck deer startled me merely by standing silently, staring in my direction. Our eyes met; he moved slowly across the road and gracefully cleared the fence before blending into the forest.

I looked both ways but neither saw nor heard any sign of a car, so I climbed the fence and walked a few yards across the field to the foot of a huge pine tree. I opened my old suitcase and scattered the contents, mostly dirty clothes, on the pine needles and lay down, instantly falling asleep. The sun was dipping near the western horizon when I woke. I sat up, leaned against the tree and smoked a cigarette. What to do? Should I go home broke and admit to Mom and Dad what had happened? Or should I get a job and forget about school?

What difference would it make whether or not I went home? What if I just got a job out here somewhere and wrote Mom and Dad a letter. They'd understand, wouldn't they? No. No, they certainly would not. So what if I go home, finish school, get educated, and then get a job. What's the difference? A better job? Maybe. Would I be happier? Maybe, maybe not. People don't get happier from better jobs, and they don't get happier from making themselves smarter – maybe just the opposite. So why all the effort? Because most people think it's our duty to make use of whatever ability God has given us. What difference does it make what people think? You want to be liked? You want to be respected? Did I? Yeah, I guess. I guess most people want to be liked and respected if they can, even if they don't admit it. But you don't have to be smart and have a better job to be liked and respected, do you?

I stood, stretched, ground out the cigarette, then threw my things in the suitcase. I'm goin' home to Bradleyville, my hometown.

Somewhere in southern Oregon, a big eighteen-wheeler picked me up. The bleary-eyed driver looked at me as I crawled in the cab.

"My name's Smokey. Can you drive this rig?" he asked. "I been running for twenty-four hours. My relief driver didn't show up, and I gotta get this load to Salt Lake by tomorrow morning. Can you drive?" he asked again, somewhat impatiently.

"Yeah, I can drive a truck. Never drove one exactly like this one, but if you'll show me the gears and stuff, I can drive her."

The exhausted driver showed me the gears, trailer brakes, tachometer, and other things he thought important. "You got eighty thousand pounds of dynamite on this baby, so be careful. It don't stop on a dime."

He took the passenger's seat and watched as I adjusted the seat and pulled the big truck and trailer onto the highway. It had a lot more gears than anything I had ever driven and was longer – much longer – and heavier – much heavier. I had driven Dad's truck at home since I was twelve and had driven wheat harvest trucks. I knew the main thing was to take it easy and to think. It wasn't long until the big diesel engine was hummin' down the highway. Smokey gave me a toothless grin, crawled over the back seat into the sleeper and yelled, "Good night, Irene!"

A few hours later we pulled into a Utah truck stop, and Smokey bought us a big breakfast of bacon, eggs, biscuits and gravy with lots of hot coffee. He bragged on my drivin' and gave me $5 as a sign of appreciation. We were going in different directions, so I had my thumb in the air again.

Hitchhiking that year was difficult, particularly after some maniac hitchhiker in Oklahoma had killed a family of five. I managed to get some short rides but was still in Utah, at yet another small town, when it began to get dark. I knew it would be difficult to get a ride after nightfall; besides, I was sleepy. A motel room would cost money, so I hit upon a plan. I walked to the Greyhound bus station, which was a part of the corner drug store.

"When's the next bus come through, goin' east?" I asked the middle-aged lady behind the counter.

"Ten-thirty tonight. Where you want to go?" she asked.

"Wherever the bus will be about daylight tomorrow morning," I answered.

She looked at a schedule and a map on the counter. "Looks to me like it'll be at Lamar, Colorado, about six in the morning," she said, pointing to the town's location on the map.

"How much is a ticket to that place?" I asked.

"Twelve dollars and fifty cents, plus tax. You want one?"

"Yeah, gimme a ticket to daylight."

A week later I sat in Mr. Watson's class at Bradleyville High School. He was a worldly man who had married a local girl in college and came to our little community from Chicago, never quite accepted, and never quite accepting. He taught sociology and talked that day about cultures.

"The problem with living in such a small, closed community," he said, "is that you folks never get more than fifty miles from home. You never get to experience the excitement of seeing how others live."

I wondered what ever happened to Jeanne.

15

MY DAD AND MY FATHER

My dad standing in his Bradleyville grocery store.

Though my dad let the fire in the old wood stove burn down, it still threw out plenty of heat. Radiant warmth from the burning wood felt good on my back that cold Friday November evening. Darkness signaled closing time, and the two of us were alone in the small general store that was our family business. I had just arrived home for the weekend after starting my freshman year in college. Dad sat behind me on the other side of the stove, on the loafer's bench. He had turned out the lights so as not to encourage some late arriving customer. Twilight darkness was broken only by the glare from the fire.

Dad had always been more like a best friend than a father. I looked forward to seeing him; he was good company because we felt at ease with each other. On this winter evening, however, I could tell he was a little restless, almost nervous. For a man with his sense of humor and easygoing manner, such demeanor seemed out of character.

My back was still turned to him when he spoke my name in a tone that let me know something special was about to happen. "Leon, there is something I've been meanin' to talk to you about for a long time," he said. "Maybe I should have done it before now. I know you've already found out about it." He was stalling, and his voice sounded a little choked. "I'm not really your dad. Me and your ma took you when you were two years old, after your real dad and mom died."

"I know, Dad," I said, trying to spare his pain.

"They lived in Colorado Springs when it happened, during the Depression. You were

My biological parents, Joe and Virgie Slone, and their first baby, Verna.

about twenty-one months old. Your dad had been a successful businessman, one of the best in this area, with lots of people working for him and plenty of money. He was honest, hardworking, and smart, but somehow the Depression and booze took him down."

With tears streaming down my face, I listened to this long-delayed story. Growing up, I had heard some rumors, mostly from schoolmates who had picked up the story from their parents, the story of how my "real" father had killed my mother and then himself. Now I was to hear the story again. Dad had worked for my biological father when he was a teenager and loved him dearly. That night he told me what a wonderful man he was, how he knew in his heart that shooting my mother had been an accident and had led to his suicide. Still I knew, and I think he knew, too, that was not true.

"Your dad was a good man. He owned several businesses here in the Ozarks. When most people were broke and half-starved, unable to make a living, he always found a way to overcome obstacles. He hired people he didn't even need because their families was hungry. He sold groceries on credit to people he knew could never pay. Despite him bein' so generous, your dad's businesses seemed to hold steady, even in the hard times of the thirties."

These positive comments were news to me. Most of what I had heard was that my mean, crazy, drunken father had killed my mother in front of me, a baby screaming in terror. Word was that a neighbor picked me up that Christmas Eve in the bloody little house and rushed me across the street to her home. I was seeing my birth father as I had never known him before.

As I listened to Dad – who had nothing to gain by praising my father – say good things about him, I could not hold back the tears. I wanted to say, "Dad, you're my hero, my one and only dad, and you don't have to tell me more." But I didn't say it, and he pressed on.

"You were the light of your mother's eye, her youngest of six. She called you her 'Church Baby' because she said she was goin' to take you to church with her, something she hadn't done as much as she would have liked with the other kids. She loved to sing hymns as she rocked you."

He told me about the funeral and how my much-older, married sister had taken me back to California. How she and her husband, with two boys of their own, were unable to support me during the hard economic times; how he and my mom had asked that I be sent back to Missouri to be their son; how an old lady brought me back on the train to Chadwick; and how the mailman brought me on to Bradleyville, a very special parcel delivery.

Then he said, "I'm proud of you, Leon, proud of how you've grown up, how you've been a good example for the three kids me and your mom had after adopting you. Joe and Jerry and Peggy look up to you, and I know you will never disappoint us. Just do what you know is right, and always do what you say you're going to. That's what your dad did, until the alcohol got him."

Not long after that night, I went back to school but soon discovered that Southwest Missouri State College was not ready for me, nor I for it. I joined the Marine Corps, served three years, and then enrolled at the University of Missouri in Columbia. To pay my way I sold what I called "Hope Chest Items," but what an old friend derisively called "pots and pans." I also sold advertising for the *Columbia Missourian,* the daily newspaper published by the School of Journalism where I studied. When a national company came to the school looking for a publisher's representative, a professor who knew of my sales experience recommended me. I got the job, the beginning and foundation of what was to become my life's work.

I worked hard and enjoyed some success on the new job, earning awards, recognition, and more money than I had ever made before, but something was not right. I felt stymied.

My career was not going anywhere. It was then that I had to face up to my most dreaded fear. Like my father before me, my problem was alcohol. Drinking had become an obsession that drowned my judgment and ambition.

In July 1966, when I walked into the basement of a small church to attend my first Alcoholics Anonymous meeting, my life took a dramatic turn. The men and women around the table in that little church basement smiled as I told "my story" because it was their story too. They didn't gloss over my problem but let me know it could be managed and that I was not alone. It hasn't been easy, but since that day in July, 1966, I have not taken a drink of alcohol.

Once I stopped drinking, I became totally committed to work, family and health. I was in a tough, competitive business, but when unusual difficulties arose, I recalled the words of my dad on that winter night. From him I had discovered that my birth father was a good businessman, and that helped me believe I could become one too.

If there is a key to my success in life and business, it is honesty and forthrightness. Simple words of my living dad and dead father have guided and anchored me throughout my business career. Of course, I am grateful that I learned sound business practices along the way, and I'm grateful for God's gift of health and for His giving me opportunities and the ability to make the most of them. Still the lesson learned standing near an old wood-burning stove in a country store in the Missouri Ozarks has made all the difference.

I left the Ozarks for forty years and thought I would never return to stay. I had learned the rhythm of the city where I built my business, raised a family, and established relationships. Yet the magnetic pull of the Ozarks drew me home. My wife and I now own a beautiful ranch where we raise Rocky Mountain elk and a herd of cattle, where we can accept my ninety-two-year-old mother's invitation for meals as only she can prepare them, and where I am in walking distance of the place where I learned the greatest lesson of my young life:

"Just do what you know is right, and always do what you say you're going to."

16

WELCOME TO MISSOURI

Early September 1957

Sondra Lee Goldman and I were married Nov. 28, 1957, a few months before this picture was taken.

Big trucks and fast-moving cars roared past me as I stood, thumb in the air, on the Hollywood Freeway of Los Angeles, hitch-hiking from the United States Marine Corps air base, El Toro, in Santa Ana, to the USO in Holly-wood. Free at last, my discharge papers and $350 in hand after serving three years in the Marines. In my pocket was a check for three hundred fifty dollars, my "mustering out" pay. My life was about to change.

Mid-afternoon sun bore down on the concrete freeway. Sweat popped out on my forehead and dampened my shirt. My seabag, containing all my personal possessions, steadily became heavier as I carried it a quarter of a mile to the top of an on-ramp where the first driver, a young Mexican in a new 1957 Chevy, screeched to a halt. He motioned me into the front seat after I threw my seabag in the back.

"Hey, Mon, where you goin'?" he asked, flashing a big smile as he floored the powerful Chevy and burned rubber entering the beehive of freeway traffic.

"Hollywood; the USO," I said, reaching to shake his hand and introduce myself.

"My name is Juan. I'm an American," he said proudly. "Born in Los Angeles. My mother and father came from Mexico."

Even though I liked to drive fast, riding with Juan was like taking my first ride on a roller coaster. The Chevy had been customized, tilted forward, with extra-wide rear tires. I noticed the "chug, chug" of the big V-8 when I got in and knew my host had "hopped up" the already powerful engine.

Juan bobbed and weaved through the heavy Friday-afternoon traffic, pushing the Chevy to its limit each time there was a bit of open space ahead. He braked, cut left and right, roared ahead, and braked again only when absolutely necessary. I could see other drivers yelling at us, favoring Juan with some unflattering finger signs. Nothing bothered him; he didn't notice irate drivers. He was too busy talking, telling me how fast his car would go – if only he had some open space to show me. I told him I believed him; he didn't have to prove it. We suddenly hit an opening in the traffic: empty highway ahead. I heard tires screaming and felt my body pressed into the seat as Juan gave full-speed-ahead orders to his powerful machine. The big Chevy responded, pushing the speedometer past one hundred in seconds.

Boy, did the USO building ever look good, especially since I thought Juan was going to kill us both on the freeway. I waved goodbye as he burned rubber and disappeared into the traffic of Hollywood Boulevard. Having survived my stint in the military and that harrowing ride, I looked forward to meeting Sondra at 4:00. Sandy, I called her, was a striking woman, tall, slender, and shapely. We had met a year earlier at the Hollywood USO, where I spent much of my time when away from El Toro. On this afternoon, Sandy appeared in an attractive blue dress with a black leather belt around her small waist, skirt held outward by a full petticoat. Black patent-leather shoes matched her belt. We were both excited about our plans to become engaged and marry soon.

We walked down Hollywood Boulevard to a jewelry store where the previous week we had looked at engagement rings. A tiny diamond on a yellow gold band looked great on Sandy's small finger. Using $110 of the government check, which the store owner cashed without hesitation, I bought the ring. That evening we sat in a booth at a small French restaurant in Hollywood, sipping champagne, holding hands, admiring the gleaming diamond on her hand.

I planned to go back to Missouri, find a small apartment, enroll in the fall semester at the University of Missouri in Columbia, and send for Sandy sometime later that fall or the next spring. As much as I loved her, I had reservations about taking this particular young woman to the Midwest. She was born and raised in Brooklyn; her family moved to Los Angeles when she was sixteen. I knew how different things were in Missouri, especially my home area in the Ozark Mountains.

Sondra Lee Goldman, Jewish. James L. Combs, Baptist. City versus country. Sophisticated opposed to unsophisticated. She was nineteen, soon to be twenty. I was twenty-two but knew our cultural and religious differences should not be overlooked when planning a life together. Yet on the most enchanting evening of my future bride's life, I did not feel it appropriate to discuss such challenges. I knew, for example, that Sandy had extreme phobias about all kinds of insects and pests. A harmless moth in the house or car would terrorize her. Just the thought of rats, mice, or cockroaches immobilized her with fear. She had never encountered the ticks and chiggers covering the hills and hollows of southwest Missouri. She talked about how much she looked forward to hiking the woods and swimming the streams of the Ozarks – without knowing what I knew. But this was not the time to blemish her dreams, so I smiled and kept quiet.

My dad and mom, Susie and Etcyl Combs, welcomed Sandy into the family.

I left California with a buddy who had also just been discharged and was driving to his home in Maryland. He gave me a free ride down Route 66 to Missouri.

A few days later I was attending class at the university, living in an upstairs room rented from an elderly lady. My only income was $110 a month from the GI Bill, so I had to take a room, which was cheaper than an apartment, until such time as Sandy could join me. I also took a night job driving a Yellow Cab in Columbia to add a few dollars a week to my meager income.

We lasted only two months before deciding Sandy should join me in Missouri. She drove her 1955 Ford across the country and arrived in Columbia two days before Thanksgiving. We planned a trip to Bradleyville to meet my parents during the holiday. Sandy was a little nervous when she saw the old Daniel Boone Hotel in Columbia where she spent the night before we drove south to my home. She asked if the hotel was clean. I knew she really meant, "Any bugs or rats?" I said it was a good place to stay – and cheap.

We obtained our marriage license before leaving Columbia the next day, then drove south to introduce Sandy to my family and enjoy Thanksgiving with them. Mom and Dad expected us. The little white farmhouse sat close to Highway 125. A woven wire fence enclosed the front yard; shade trees stood randomly, shedding colorful leaves in the November breeze. My brothers, thirteen-year-old Jerry and nine-year-old Joe, greeted the '55 Ford as we pulled off the highway. Sam, their old shepherd dog, jumped and wagged his tail frantically at the sight of company.

Mom came out on the small front porch as we stepped from the car. I grabbed Jerry and Joe, one with each arm, and gave them each a big hug as they eyed Sandy, unsure how to approach her. She solved the problem by smiling when I introduced them, extending a hand to each. They took our bags, carrying and dragging them toward the house.

Dad walked from the barn carrying a bucket of milk. Everyone stood on the small porch as I introduced Sandy to my family. Mom took her by the hand and welcomed her inside where a fire burned in the little wood-burning heat stove. The house was immaculately clean, the way my mother always kept it, and the aroma of fresh-baked bread drifted from the kitchen. Mom directed Jerry to take Sandy's suitcase into the front bedroom, a well-lighted space with two large windows trimmed with snow-white lace curtains, handmade by my mother. A beautiful custom-made quilt that my grandmother had given us served as a spread for the double bed. My mother told Sandy that was her room. I would sleep on the divan.

Thanksgiving dinner decorated the table that evening, although the holiday was the next day. Golden fried chicken filled a large platter. Mashed potatoes, gravy, corn, green beans and steaming hot rolls covered every square inch of space on the white, starched tablecloth. Two chocolate pies, my favorite, sat on the kitchen counter next to an angel food cake. A big bowl of red strawberries, freshly thawed from the freezer, brightened the scene.

I told my family that Sandy and I planned to get married the next day in Springfield. We didn't know where but would find a preacher and do it. They were not surprised since they already knew my intentions. We talked about Sandy's drive from California, my classes at the university, and what was going on with my family.

Sandy helped Mom clean the table and wash dishes after dinner. They hit it off right away and began a long family friendship, bonding as only women do.

We gathered in the family room, a small living area with a large divan and two comfortable chairs, Dad's and Mom's. Jerry and Joe lounged on the floor as we talked about Sandy's life in New York and California. My parents asked questions about her mother and father. Sandy and I sat on the divan, not as close as we would have liked, making every effort to behave respectfully.

In the midst of this pleasant conservation, Dad suddenly yelled, "Jerry, there he goes. Head him off!" He dropped to the floor on all fours. Jerry and Joe immediately took up positions on hands and knees. A mouse raced down the wall and stopped in the corner. Sandy's shriek was lost amid the clamor. She jerked her feet from the floor and tucked them beneath her on the divan.

"Get over by the wall, Jerry!" Dad yelled frantically. "Joe, stay in the middle. I'll come down this wall. Get your hands down, Jerry! Don't let him get by. Move up, Joe. Get closer." All three crouched, edging toward the terrified, cornered mouse. I'd often heard the expression, "like a cornered rat," and now I knew what it meant. Sandy gripped my arm with one hand while chewing the knuckles of the other, speechless.

The little furry creature backed farther into the corner, beady eyes darting left and right. He started down the wall toward Jerry. Stopped, then back to the corner, then down Dad's wall. The mouse stopped. It looked up the middle toward Joe. They all edged closer.

Mom spoke apologetically, "They've been trying to get that mouse for a week. Tried traps, poison, everything." Sandy didn't hear. Her transfixed stare never left the mouse. She was hurting my arm, and I thought she might bite her hand too hard. I tried to remove it from her mouth, but her muscles stiffened and quivered.

Jerry charged the corner, panicking the mouse, sending him down Dad's wall. A big burly hand slammed down on the little ball of fur and came up with the mouse pinched between thumb and forefinger. The big squeeze produced one final pathetic squeak. Dad laughed and Jerry and Joe jumped up and down triumphantly as he walked outside and threw the dead mouse across the yard fence.

Sandy buried her head in my chest. I realized she had been biting her hand to stifle screams. Mom was the only one who noticed her agony. She came over to the divan and told me to move. Sitting down by Sandy, she took my future bride in her arms. My mother wiped tears away as they rolled down Sandy's cheeks. Jerry and Joe wondered what was the matter as Dad rejoiced and walked to the bathroom to wash his hands.

Always a good sport, Sandy soon recovered and forced a little laugh at the mousecapade.

"I've never seen that before," she said, trying to explain her reaction.

After another big Thanksgiving dinner the next day, we drove to Springfield, found a Baptist preacher named Truman Dollar and were married. We stood in his private quarters, his wife as witness, and took our vows. I gave him $13, two day's pay for a part-time taxi driver. Sandy looked beautiful in a pretty white dress she had bought in California for the occasion. We went to a little Chinese restaurant on St. Louis Avenue for our wedding dinner and spent our one-night honeymoon at the Skyline Motel on Glenstone Boulevard in Springfield.

Back in Columbia the next day we walked down the stairs to our little forty-dollar-a-month basement apartment. It was dark and damp, but we lightened the place up and filled it with joy, after I convinced Sandy there were no mice in the place.

17

THE COCKFIGHTER

Excitement radiated from Lonnie Taber's voice as he drove down the highway, telling me about the sport of cockfighting. We were headed to Oklahoma that Saturday morning for one of the biggest cockfights of the year, where he would match his roosters against the best in the business. He told me how he bred fighting roosters, how he fed and cared for them, and how he "got rid" of the no-good ones.

"Ol' Hillbilly's gonna be there today, I know," he said. "He's a big ol' boy from Oklahoma – Indian, I think, but he dresses and talks funny. That's why we all call him 'Hillbilly.' He's got some real good fightin' chickens – whipped mine last time – but I'm

Lonnie Taber holds one of his fighting cocks.

layin' for him today." Enthusiasm drove his conversation; love of the sport lit up his fifty-three-year-old freckled face with smiles. "I didn't have ol' Post Maul with me last time – left him back to heal from his last fight – but he'll be there today. I guarantee you, Hillbilly don't have a rooster that'll kill Ol' Post Maul."

"Tell me about Post Maul," I said. "Where is he now?"

"Ol' Rodney took all my birds down there early this morning. Ol' Post Maul's the fightin'est damned rooster in this part of the country. I call him Post Maul 'cause when he hits another rooster, it's like drivin' a fence post with a post maul – a sledgehammer, you know. He's already won fifteen fights – killed ever' one of 'em, and I'm tellin' you he's a mean S.O.B. He likes me though – knows I'm his master – the one that feeds him. He's made me at least $5,000 on prize money and bets. I wouldn't sell him for that right now. Ol' Post Maul will make Hillbilly want to get in his old beat-up truck and go home." He smiled and gripped the steering wheel tighter, knuckles turning white in anticipation.

We turned south off the main highway onto a dusty gravel road, winding through some fields and entering a wooded area. Tall trees on both sides leaned across the road, forming a tunnel. A mile later we came upon a clearing filled with pickups, rifles in back windows; small campers; and cars. A large barn-like structure sat on the corner of the clearing.

"That's Rooster Arena," Taber said. "They got a good crowd. There's ol' Hillbilly's truck. See it, that old gray GMC with chicken coops on the back. He's here. I knowed he'd be here."

We parked and went inside, paying our ten-dollar admission fee to a heavyset woman at the front door. Taber arranged reserved seats, second row from the fighting pits. He wanted me to have a good spot for my first cockfight. He wore cowboy boots, a big western hat, and a smile; everybody knew and liked him. "Hey, Cowboy, who'd you bring with you, there?" asked a tall, skinny man, a cigarette dangling from his lips. "He somebody to help carry your dead chickens home?" Others chimed in with good-natured teasing, but I could tell they respected Taber's reputation and knowledge of cockfighting. He found our seats, then left to check his roosters.

Rooster Arena resembled a livestock sale barn, featuring good theater-type seats to accommodate 750 guests surrounding a fifteen-foot-square fighting pit in the middle of the floor. Two-foot-high wooden walls enclosed the pit, and mesh wire extended upward another four feet. Other than a dirt floor, the pit resembled a boxing ring with an old fluorescent light suspended directly overhead.

The cockfighters association held a benefit auction in the pit before the derby started. I watched the auction while Taber checked his roosters. A little man wearing overalls, sitting behind me, leaned forward to say, "They raise money for lawyers to keep the government and bleedin'-heart liberals off our backs. That's what the auction's for." I watched the neophyte auctioneer walk around the pit taking bids on trios of chickens. Three wire cages sat in the center of the pit, each containing a cock and two hens – a trio. The auctioneer, microphone in one hand, cigarette in the other, wore striped overalls, side buttons undone, and a feed company ball cap pushed to the back of his head.

Roosters crowed from every direction, including the trios being auctioned. Their beautiful plumes added brilliance to the otherwise drab surroundings. Almost everyone smoked. A young woman in the row ahead of me, cigarette dangling from her lips, combed her little girl's hair. A layer of smoke drifted through the arena, forming a small cloud above the pit. Coughing and hacking from the audience punctuated the auctioneer's appeal for bids.

Everyone looked to my left toward a rustle of activity. A huge man wearing bib overalls and a red, white and blue shirt resembling a flag walked toward the pit. Though he stood six-foot-six and weighed almost four hundred pounds, he moved with the grace of an athlete. The flag shirt was cut off at the shoulders revealing massive hairy arms and hands.

Long, thick black hair fell over his shoulders, and a black John L. Sullivan mustache made a huge slash mark across his face. His belly pushed the overalls out in front. He looked like a weight lifter, and he didn't smile.

"That's ol' Hillbilly," the old fellow behind me said. "He's a tough old boy; got some real good roosters. He usually wins here. He's an Indian. Some says he lives in a teepee."

Hillbilly strode past the ring, nodding to a couple of bird owners, and started toward the back of the arena where the roosters were cooped.

Returning from his chickens, Lonnie Taber met face-to-face with the big man.

"Hey, Cowboy, I thought I learnt you a lesson last time. Didn't think you'd have any of them measly roosters left after my birds kilt most of 'em," Hillbilly roared.

"How you doin', son?" Taber said to the big man.

"You got any decent roosters this time?" Hillbilly asked. "I feel bad about wipin' you out of business. Maybe you ought to quit and come work for me." Though Taber had lost several birds to Hillbilly the previous year, Hillbilly still stung after losing most of his birds to Taber's cocks two years earlier.

Taber smiled and clasped the man's big hand, "Son, I've got a surprise for you today. Do you still have Elvis?"

"'Course I do. He ain't lost a fight in his life. Killed nineteen cocks. Why?"

"How much would you be willin' to bet on old Elvis? I got a cock I think can whoop him." Taber said, smiling, looking the big man in the eye. Elvis, like ol' Post Maul, was known far and wide. Other cockfighters wanted his offspring for breeding. He was a Hatch breed; Post Maul, an Oriental Asil.

"You must be talkin' about that Asil rooster of yours," Hillbilly said, "I ain't seen him, but I tell you right now, he can't kill my cock. I got two hundred fifty dollars that says he can't. Whatta you think of that?"

"Is that all you think of Old Elvis? How 'bout five hundred dollars and we'll talk to Old Jake and start the day off with a match fight – your bird against mine." Jake owned the arena. A crowd gathered around the two men, both experts in cockfights, both gamblers, both lovers of the game. A tiny, red-headed woman stood beside Hillbilly, wearing skin-tight jeans and a tight, black T-shirt, a beautiful rooster on front, the word "Elvis" inscribed above the picture and "The King" below. Hillbilly's girlfriend.

"Kick his ass, Hon," she said to Hillbilly. "Kill his stupid bird and take his money." Elvira also remembered Taber's roosters.

"Shut up, Elvira," Hillbilly said. "Just keep your mouth shut." He turned to Taber. "Just how much cash you got on you, Cowboy. Let's get serious. How 'bout a thousand dollars? Think you can scrape up that much?"

"You're on. You want knives or gaffs?" Taber asked. Gaffs are pinpoint-sharp steel spurs fastened to each leg of the rooster, allowing him to stab his opponent. Knives, more deadly than gaffs, are four inches long, razor sharp and fastened to the left leg only.

"Gaffs," Hillbilly said. "That way maybe your chicken will last at least a minute or two. You got the money? I don't want no credit."

"Don't worry about the money, son. I got the money, but you won't get it 'cause you're gonna be carryin' out a dead rooster. Let's go tell Jake and get our roosters."

"Hey, Cowboy," Elvira's shrill voice sounded above crowing cocks. "Hope you've made your truck payments, 'cause you ain't gonna have no money left when Hillbilly gets through with you."

Taber ignored her.

Jake approved the plan; the men went to get their fighting cocks. Three hundred people milled around the pits, taking bets, writing in little notebooks, talking excitedly about the match fight.

"Hundred even on Cowboy," or "Lay eighty," they shouted across the arena, meaning someone wanted to bet one hundred dollars against eighty on Elvis.

A nine-year-old boy jumped from his seat and yelled, "Twenty on Cowboy! Twenty even on Cowboy." His father, a red bandana around his head, watched proudly as someone took his son's bet. Other bets were matched. Finally, Jake's wife spoke on the public-address system.

"We're startin' off with a match fight today. Hillbilly and Cowboy will fight their roosters. Now, I don't want to have to tell you people today to throw your dead chickens in the trash. Last week some of you left them in the hallways. Don't do it no more."

A farmer sat on the front row, dozing. He wore an American-flag cap, overalls and plaid shirt, hands clasped loosely over belly. A plastic pencil holder held half a dozen pens and pencils in his bib pocket. Someone behind shook his shoulder, "Ed, fifty dollars on Hillbilly?"

"Okay," the farmer said, then dozed off again.

People stood as Taber and Hillbilly emerged from the back door of the arena carrying their roosters. Elvis looked tiny cradled in Hillbilly's huge right arm. The big man's left hand encircled the bird's neck to keep him from getting loose. Taber followed, holding Ol' Post Maul the same way. Post Maul sighted Elvis and struggled to get free, to attack. His beautiful, long tail feathers reached halfway to the ground from Taber's arm. The sight of the roosters increased the level of betting and yelling.

"Call forty-five, call forty-five," the sleepy farmer said as he awoke with a start.

"Hundred even," the little man behind me countered. "I want Hillbilly."

"Bet," the sleepy farmer said, scribbling in his note pad.

"Twenty on Cowboy! Twenty on Cowboy," the nine-year-old tried to get another bet.

"Get the hell outta the way," Elvira screamed, trying to make way for Hillbilly to get to the pit. "For Christ's sake, let us through."

"Shut up, Elvira," Hillbilly roared above the crowd, his massive body following the little woman.

Elvira turned to Taber, "Your old rooster looks pretty beat up to me, Cowboy, like maybe he's seen his best days." She got too close and ol' Post Maul tried to peck her.

A woman's tough voice on the PA system broke in, "If you people don't get outta the aisles and in your seat, I ain't gonna let this fight start. Now set down!"

The crowd gradually settled down, but the bet-shouting continued.

Hillbilly and Taber stepped into the pit. Ol' Post Maul surprised Taber with a loud crow, unusual for a rooster while being held. Elvis responded immediately, as if to say, "I'm ready." The gamecocks struggled to get at each other, feathers raised on their necks, but the handlers held tight.

The referee spat tobacco juice to the side. He wore sunglasses despite the dim lights. Faded jeans barely clung to his bony hips. After checking the birds' steel gaffs, he used a stick to draw lines in the dirt eight feet apart, directing Taber to one, Hillbilly to the other.

"Okay," the ref said, "Build 'em up." Taber and Hillbilly held their birds and moved close, head to head, swaying back and forth, allowing the warriors to peck each other furiously. Their fearless eagerness to attack marked both birds as champions, each undefeated, never failing to kill their opponents. They were pure fighters, bred and born to kill, their life's mission: kill, kill now, kill fast. Hillbilly towered over Taber as they swayed back and forth, shoving their birds at the other, building them up for the fight to the death. The cocks struggled and strained in their owners' hands. The handlers' hearts raced in time with their gladiators. Elvis crowed again, and ol' Post Maul answered before he finished, fighting to free himself from Taber's grip.

"Ready!" shouted the skinny referee. The handlers backed up to the eight-foot lines and lowered their birds' feet to the ground. They continued to restrain them until the referee shouted, "Pit your cocks!" The released killer warriors raced headlong at each other.

The fighting roosters held their heads low as they raced toward each other, only to raise them for a head-on crash at center-pit, wings beating wildly, feathers flying everywhere, to the frenzied shouts and screams from the crowd. True to his name, Ol' Post Maul hit Elvis so hard he knocked him back a foot or two. Hillbilly's bird reacted frantically, slashing at Post Maul with his steel spurs. They rolled in the dust, pecking viciously spurring, squawking.

Just as their roosters were experienced veterans, so were the handlers. Taber and Hillbilly stood close to their birds, arms hanging, ready to grab when the referee called, "Handle your cocks." Obviously, both were excellent trainers who had well-fed, highly trained fighting machines. Knowing how to handle their roosters in the pit is critical; a handler mistake can doom a bird to certain death.

"Kill him, Elvis!" Elvira screamed. "Kill the son of a bitch!"

"Get back, Elvira!" the referee yelled. "Get away from the pit!"

"Get him, Post Maul!" the nine-year-old yelled as he crowded near the pit.

The sleepy farmer, now awake, leaned forward, hands on knees.

Sweat poured from Hillbilly. The Indian's giant body dwarfed the surroundings. He shouted instructions to Elvis between clenched teeth. Taber spoke softly to ol' Post Maul, staying close, ready to handle his bird.

"Bang." The two birds collided. Elvis spurred Taber's bird and they went down.

"Handle your cocks!" yelled the ref. The roosters lay motionless. The handlers quickly put hands on their birds, holding them gently. "Unhang 'em!" the referee yelled. Taber carefully removed the steel spur from ol' Post Maul and carried him back to the eight-foot line. Hillbilly held Elvis on his line while the ref slowly counted to ten. Taber checked his bird and decided the wound was not deadly. He held ol' Post Maul's head next to his cheek as the rooster panted, eyes on Elvis. "Get 'im, old boy," Taber whispered to his fighter.

"Pit your cocks!" the skinny referee yelled. The roosters raced at each other. This time ol' Post Maul ducked as Elvis went airborne over him, then Taber's rooster pounced on Elvis, ramming a spur into his side, hammering it home with beating wings.

"Handle your cocks!" yelled the ref, and the handlers picked up their birds.

Bettors and onlookers stood, screaming encouragement. Some crowded around the pit, provoking Jake's wife again, "Hey, you people! How many times I gotta tell you, get the hell back from the pit."

The cockfight continued, neither old warrior giving an inch, blood pouring from both their beaks. They fought to exhaustion, barely able to stand, but still aching to kill. Taber talked to ol' Post Maul in low tones when he handled him, almost whispering, to an old friend. The rooster knew his job and never took his eye off Elvis.

I worried. Taber's prize rooster was in the fight of his life, and Taber had a thousand dollars riding on the outcome. His bird looked game, but it also looked hurt. I knew Taber had the money, but I also knew he couldn't afford to lose it. Just as ol' Post Maul was a fighter, however, Taber was a gambler. "Ain't no gamble if you know you're gonna win," he would say. I watched during a pause as he held his bird to his mouth, blew gently on his back feathers, and wiped blood from his head. The rooster never stopped concentrating, but when Taber set him on the pit floor seconds before the fight was to resume, the rooster staggered, then regained his balance. As if to disguise that little stagger, the beautiful cock looked at Elvis, threw his chest out, his head back, and crowed, a true warrior, drowning the shouts in Rooster Arena. Elvis didn't respond this time. He breathed hard and seemed disoriented when Hillbilly put him on the ground.

"Pit your cocks," the ref said, this time in a quieter voice. The cocks moved slowly, circling each other, heads bobbing up and down with their opponent's. Elvis pounced, wings in a flurry, landing atop Post Maul. He grabbed the back of Post Maul's neck in his strong, sharp beak and hung on, dragging the cock in a circle. Taber's rooster managed to get loose but now looked confused. Post Maul didn't seem to know where Elvis was, and Hillbilly's rooster, sensing a kill, rammed a steel spur in the bird's side.

"Handle your cocks!" The owners held their birds firmly on the dirt floor while Taber again removed the steel spike from his fighting cock.

"Hey, Cowboy!" Elvira yelled, "wanna double your bet," then she cackled like a chicken. Taber ignored her.

"I'll betya another twenty on Post Maul!" the nine-year-old screamed.

"You got yourself a bet, Kid," the little woman answered.

That's it, I thought. Post Maul's done for. I caught Taber's eye as he massaged his bird, wiping more blood from the rooster's head. Taber winked and showed a tiny smile. Elvis crowed, sensing another kill. Post Maul didn't respond. He staggered again when Taber put him on the ground, but once again he turned toward Elvis and charged when the ref yelled, "Pit!" The charge was slow, both birds physically exhausted, but their fighting spirit remained as strong as ever. Elvis knocked Post Maul down and grabbed his head again, yanking, ripping.

Ol' Post Maul, flat on his back, saw his opening. Elvis's wings were spread as he stood atop Post Maul, viciously pecking his head. Post Maul slammed both spurs into Elvis' sides, driving them home with beating wings.

"Handle your cocks!" the ref yelled. Both birds lay motionless in the dirt. The crowd hushed. Handlers held the birds gently while Hillbilly removed first one gaff, then the other from his prize cock. Ol' Post Maul, almost lifeless in Taber's hands, raised his head and crowed weakly, holding his head high, and then slumped into his master's arm. He raised his head and turned toward Taber as if to ask, "How'm I doin'?"

Hillbilly held a limp bird in his huge hands. The ref looked closely at the cock, and then looked again. "This cock's dead," he said, pointing at Elvis. "This cock's the winner," pointing to Post Maul. Silence for a moment, then cheers and jeers erupted. The crowd watched as Hillbilly and Elvira stared at Elvis. I saw sweat streaming down Hillbilly's face, especially near his eyes. He reached into his pocket, pulled out a fat wallet and handed it to Elvira. She counted out ten one-hundred-dollar bills, walked across the pit and silently shoved them into Taber's hand. No words from her.

"Thanks, Elvira; sorry about Elvis."

Taber stood with the money in his left hand, Ol' Post Maul in his right, and watched as his valiant rooster died. Ol' Post Maul died undefeated.

18

MY NEIGHBOR, BIRDLE

The Mannons, from left, Elnora, Mrs. Mannon and Birdle, taken in 1965, walked everywhere.

Bill Varner, a reporter from *USA Today* in Washington, D.C., was on the other end of the phone on that cold and dreary Friday afternoon in December 1996. I sat in my little farmhouse ranch office as he explained how a friend had told him about "an old woman of the Missouri Ozarks" named Birdle Mannon. Bill wrote for the national newspaper and wanted to come to our little town to do a story on the "old woman."

"Do you know anything about Birdle?" I asked.

"Just what my friend told me, that she lives back in the wilderness all by herself, with no electricity or indoor plumbing," he responded.

"You've got that part right," I said. "What are you proposing?"

"I want to come down there and interview her," he said.

"When?"

"Day after tomorrow," he said without hesitation. "Do you think she will see me?"

I told Varner I would check with Birdle and call him back. I called her on her partyline telephone, her only concession to the twentieth century, and told her about the reporter. "Would you mind if I brought him over Sunday?" I asked.

She hesitated, then said, "No, I don't mind if you'll be with him."

I assured her I would be with him and would call again before we came over. I also told her it might be a little after dark Sunday evening and asked if that would be okay. She said it would, so I relayed the message to Bill in Washington.

"I'll be there Sunday," he said.

I told him he could stay in our guest house, but he insisted he would stay in a local motel.

"Not around here, you won't," I said. "No motels in Bradleyville, nothing for thirty miles." Hearing that, he agreed to stay in the little farmhouse we kept for guests.

Bill Varner was a city boy, never having wandered far from New York, Washington and other eastern urban centers up and down the coast. He rented a car at the Springfield airport and found his way down hilly, winding Highway 125 to Bradleyville and finally to our little house on Beaver Creek Elk and Cattle Ranch.

My wife Dot and I talked about Birdle during dinner at our house. Bill was impressed when I told him the steak he was enjoying was homegrown right here on the ranch. He asked how long we had known Birdle, how old she was, why she lived alone back in the woods. While intentionally extending dinner, waiting for darkness, I told him we were going to see her after dinner so he could ask her those questions.

We finished our meal. "Ready to go?"

He jumped up and said, "We can take my rental car."

"It won't make it over the road to Birdle's," I said. "We'll have to take my truck."

We climbed into the twenty-year-old powder-blue Chevy pickup with a huge crack in the windshield, hood tied down with bailing wire and one headlight out. Cold wind howled through the pitch darkness, bending the huge maple tree in our front yard and rocking my old pickup as we drove toward Birdle's cabin. We turned off the highway onto a rough dirt and gravel road, which became almost impassable as we topped Dick Bald, one of the highest hills around. I drove in low gear, easing through icy mud holes and over boulders that formed the roadbed.

Bill edged to the front of his seat looking anxiously left and right and over his shoulder. I stopped, turned off the engine and lights, and rolled down the window.

"What are you doing?" Bill asked nervously.

"Just wanted to listen to see what we can hear," I said. "Roll down your window."

Silence. Though we were a foot or two apart, I could barely make out his outline. Then a pack of coyotes cut loose, yelping, howling, barking. They sounded very close.

"What's that?" Bill asked, obviously uncomfortable.

"Just a pack of coyotes."

"Are they dangerous?" he asked, rolling up his window.

"Nah, they're harmless," I said, starting up the old truck. We drove slowly over the rough road as tree limbs and brush crowded us more and more until finally we were barely able to see the road. The one weak headlight did little to show us the way on the very dark night. Larger limbs scraped the hood and sides of the pickup. A recent heavy rainstorm had washed big ditches in the road, making certain spots almost impassable, but the four-wheel drive slowly pushed ahead.

A large limb lay across the road. I stopped, set the emergency brake and told Bill he would have to help me move it.

"Are there any dangerous wild animals in these woods?" he asked, slowly stepping out of the truck.

"Oh, yeah, a few, I guess," I said casually. "People say they see an occasional mountain lion or a black bear once in a while. Lots of bobcats around, but they won't hurt you." He didn't seem convinced and kept glancing over his shoulder.

As he took hold of the tree limb, he turned to a sudden loud rustling in the leaves off the road. Bill saw something; he yelled, throwing up his arms, running toward me, stumbling as he looked back.

"It's only Maggie," I said. "It's our dog." Maggie, a big, friendly, gray-wolf look-alike, came charging across the road, wagging her tail furiously. She had followed us from the house. Bill recovered; we moved the limb out of the road, put Maggie in the back and continued down the long hill toward Birdle's cabin.

The farther we went, the worse the road. The reporter leaned forward anxiously, his head almost touching the windshield, looking left and right for "wild animals."

A hundred yards from Birdle's cabin, we forded a small branch, running fast and full from the recent rain. Naked trees allowed us to see the dim light of Birdle's window. "Is that her house?" Bill asked, almost whispering. "I see someone in the window – is that her?"

I stopped again and turned off the engine. We couldn't see the outline of her cabin, but we could see the window, dimly lit by her kerosene lamp. As in an Alfred Hitchcock movie, we saw the hunched-over form of an old woman, silhouetted against the lamplight. Bill was breathing heavy. His questions began again. "Who takes care of her? Isn't she afraid? What if she gets sick?"

The four-wheel-drive pulled us up the steep incline, the one headlight flashing on a rusty woven-wire-fenced yard and a huge black walnut tree. I parked.

"Let's go," I said. Bill stumbled on something and almost fell in the darkness. He cringed as I banged hard on the homemade wooden door, yelling "Birdle!" as loud as I could. No response. Her hearing was very bad. I continued, hammering with my fist, shouting her name, until finally she opened the door.

"Come in," Birdle said in her high-pitched voice, as she wrestled with the stubborn door. We stepped inside the tiny dark room, lighted by the lone kerosene lamp, casting eerie shadows onto the wobbly floor of loose boards covered with worn linoleum. An old dog gave us a surly look, then crawled under a daybed.

A Bible lay open next to the lamp on Birdle's only table.

"Here are chairs. Pull 'em up close to the stove so we can keep warm," she said as she arranged her chair so that we sat in a tiny circle, knees almost touching. "I just put in a big stick of wood so we can talk." She wore an old, long dress, high-topped shoes, granny glasses and a head scarf tied under her chin. Deep wrinkles lined her face.

Bill was still speechless, taking in everything in the tiny frontier home. I began the conversation, speaking loudly so she could hear. "Birdle, thank you for letting us come over this evening. Bill works for a national newspaper and wants to write a story about your life."

She smiled and looked at him. "That's okay, but I don't know why anyone would be interested in me. I haven't done anything worthy of such attention."

She looked at Bill. He squirmed and said, "Ma'am, lots of people will be interested in your life."

"What! What'd he say?" she turned to me.

"Talk louder, Bill," I said.

He repeated, then we began asking questions. In flawless English and remarkable memory despite her eighty-seven years, she began her story with her family's trip from North Platte, Nebraska, to Missouri in 1916 when she was seven years old. She told how her father, Samuel Mannon, built a covered wagon for the journey. A pair of oxen pulled the wagon loaded with the Mannon family and all their possessions. Her mother, Thea, let the children ride while she often walked beside Samuel. Birdle, her sister, Elnora, and brothers, Miles and Halley, were all nine years old and younger.

From left, are Thea Mannon, who lived to be ninety-five; Elnora and Birdle.

Bill Varner planned to stay in our guest house four nights and hoped to visit Birdle each day. He asked if he could come back over the next day for more conversation. She said that would be fine, so we left after about an hour.

"I hate to leave her all alone," Bill said as we drove away.

"It's her life, Bill. It's what she loves," I said.

Back at our house, Bill was still in a mild state of shock. I asked if he thought there was a story in Birdle.

"A story! My goodness, yes. It'll be a front-page story."

Dot said, "How could they put that kind of story on the front page – it's not news."

"It will be on the front page, and it will be good," Bill Varner said without sounding the least bit doubtful. We traded vehicles – my old pickup for his rental car so he could get back to Birdle's the next day.

The *USA Today* reporter stayed four days as originally planned and spent a good part of each day with Birdle. He sat with her in her little shack, took her for drives as she told stories about various places in the vicinity, and he drove her to Jim's One-Stop in Bradleyville for groceries.

Bill usually came by my office at the end of each day, always more fascinated by Birdle than the day before, telling me things I already knew. What seemed to puzzle him most was that such an intelligent, educated woman would choose to spend her life in isolation, tucked away deep in a valley of the Ozarks, happy to go weeks at a time without seeing another human being.

The Mannon family was poor but proud when they left Nebraska for Missouri in 1916. Samuel heard of cheap land with plenty of trees that could be used to build a log house and for firewood. Freshwater streams abounded in the Ozarks; fish and wild game flourished. Oxen pulled the covered wagon slowly in a southeasterly direction, Samuel walking and driving the oxen while Thea and the children rode. An old horse, tied to the wagon, plodded along behind. After traveling at a snail's pace for weeks, they passed through Springfield, Missouri, and continued to the tiny village of Chadwick. A friend had told Samuel he could get him a job at a tomato-canning factory there.

The family lived in the wagon at Chadwick several weeks while Samuel earned a few dollars then moved on to Bradleyville after he put a down payment on one hundred sixty acres of wilderness land near that small village. He agreed to pay $400 over a period of years for the land covered with cold-water springs and timber.

The first winter was especially difficult for the family. Samuel built a makeshift residence from an old, abandoned, roofless farmhouse, covering it with boards he found at another site. Guy Floyd, one of their nearest neighbors, who lived three miles away, brought the family a cured ham a couple of days before Thanksgiving and was surprised when Samuel politely informed him that the family ate no meat, a practice of their religion. The Mannons had brought some fruits and vegetables with them, some canned in fruit jars and others in bushel baskets. They stocked up on canned tomatoes Samuel accepted instead of cash for some of his labor at Chadwick. Other neighbors brought food and help to the strange family from Nebraska.

Old-timers describe the family as "different" but nice, poor but proud, near starvation but trusting wholeheartedly in God. Samuel Mannon tanned leather and made his own shoes partly because he had no money, but more likely because he had a clubfoot in need of custom fitting. He loved the natural beauty of the Ozarks hills and painted pictures of trees, plants and wild flowers. His coonskin cap and chest-length beard gave him the look of a true pioneer, a self-sufficient man of God, who lived by faith and the sweat of his brow.

Thea Mannon planted a garden and fruit trees; she canned wild fruit and garden vegetables, storing them in the cellar Samuel made. An educated woman, she insisted her children attend the little Brownbranch School regularly, and she augmented their learning by teaching them at home. The Holy Bible served as the family's main source of literature, inspiration and faith.

With help and kindness of neighbors, the family survived the winter of 1916; then Samuel built a small log cabin the next spring and summer. The children wandered through the hills picking wild berries, hunting mushrooms and gathering nuts.

Little six-year-old Halley, born in 1910, was named after Halley's Comet that crossed the skies that year. Samuel was impressed. Not only did he name his newborn son after the comet but he also painted a picture of it streaking across the heavens as it does every seventy-six years. Halley loved to crack and eat black walnuts gathered that first autumn from the nearest black walnut tree almost half a mile from the cabin. In the fall of 1916 he dropped a black walnut in the corner of their yard, pressed it into the ground with his heel and said, "Now, someday I'll have my own walnut tree." The giant eighty-seven-year-old tree from Halley's black walnut seed stands eighty-five-feet tall in the corner of the yard today, but Little Halley died that winter of 1917, a victim of the influenza epidemic that swept the country.

The Mannons adjusted to and fell in love with the harsh hills of Southwest Missouri, enduring hardships, never complaining. Bridles's other brother, Miles, became a preacher, walking from tiny church to tiny church delivering the word of God. On one particularly long trek to a church, he spent the night in the woods, sleeping on a pile of leaves. It rained all night, soaking him to the bone, but he went on to the church and preached to the waiting faithful few. A few days later, Miles Mannon followed his little brother in death, drawing his last breath in the cabin his father had hewn from the woods. Samuel Mannon's death came in his beloved cabin during the depths of the Great Depression in the mid-thirties, leaving only the three women – Thea and her two daughters, Elnora and Birdle.

The Mannon women walked through the woods several miles to my parents' country store in Brownbranch. Even Thea, who lived to be ninety-five, walked, holding a long cane to support her miniature frame. Arthritis bent her severely so that her body from hips to head was parallel to the ground. As a young boy, I marveled at her ability to make the long walk and wondered what kept her from bumping into things, since her posture forced her to look straight down at the ground. Finally, Mrs. Mannon died too in the cabin where her sons and husband had departed this earth, leaving only Elnora and Birdle.

The Mannon girls never married, though both were intelligent, nice-looking women. Elnora, more venturesome than her sister, traveled to western states to work for cash during harvest. The sisters celebrated when Elnora earned enough to have a well drilled and hand pump installed outside their cabin. For decades they had carried water from a nearby spring.

Birdle and Elnora grew even closer after the death of their family. Birdle stabilized her more daring sister while Elnora provided Birdle with exciting stories from the outside world. They walked together to the store, to church, to funerals of neighbors. They nursed each other's illnesses, offering encouragement during life's challenges. They prevailed, trusting totally and completely in God, never doubting they would spend eternity in heaven with their Lord Jesus.

Elnora departed first, passing on to the Promised Land in 1972. It was sudden, unexpected, especially since her mother had lived to ninety-five. Birdle was crushed, even knowing her dear sister was now with the Lord. Friends bringing Birdle home from the funeral on a hot August day begged her to stay a few days with them. She refused. They offered to come in and stay with her in her cabin; she thanked them but said no.

The neighbors drove away slowly, leaving Birdle standing by the wooden yard gate her father had made many years before. She stared at the rusty hinge that had pulled loose from the post, allowing the gate to hang crooked. Slowly she crossed the yard and stepped into the little house, wondering how she could possibly go on without her beloved sister. Despair overtook her and she began to cry, facing the wall, her back to the open door.

"Someone entered the room," she told me years later. "I felt a presence, a warmth, and it was as if someone's arms wrapped gently around me. I knew it was my Lord Jesus, and I have never been lonely a minute since that day."

Bill Varner stopped at my office to say goodbye on Thursday as he headed for the Springfield airport. "Did you know," he asked, "that Birdle never heard of Elvis? Or the Beatles? Did you know that she has two years of college from Southwest Missouri State University? That she walked miles through the hills to teach in one-room schoolhouses? Did you know she loves babies and would have liked to marry and raise a family? That she won awards from the Missouri Press Association for being the best rural correspondent in the state?" He kept telling me things I knew, but he was so completely taken with Birdle that he couldn't stop. We said goodbye as he promised to let me know when the story would run.

He called on Christmas Day 1996, saying the story would be in the next day's paper. And there she was, her kindly, wrinkled face taking up almost a third of the front page of *USA Today*. A wonderful, loving story accompanied the classic photo, and Bill Varner's true affection for the "Old Woman of the Ozarks" burst forth from the page. The newspaper received thousands of letters, asking questions about Birdle. A Chicago disk jockey managed to get her phone number and called her, putting her on the air for his audience. Paul Harvey told her story to his radio audience of millions. Letters and packages arrived by the dozens, addressed only to Birdle Mannon, Bradleyville, Missouri. She read the letters, some tearfully, stacking the packages in the corner. School children sent valentines, sweaters, shawls, and gloves because they read that she had no heat, no hot water, no electric lights, no refrigerator, no television – a life unimaginable to them.

A major ice storm hit the Ozarks on New Year's Day 1999. Someone called to say that

Birdle was down from a fall on the ice as she carried wood to her stove. I went to her with First Responders, Eric Guerin and Larry Blair, in a four-wheel-drive truck equipped with chains. We carefully loaded her in the truck and took her to a waiting ambulance in Bradleyville. The ambulance took her to Skaggs Hospital in Branson where surgeons

Birdle Mannon and I stand outside her cabin.

PHOTO BY LEE ANN RUSSELL

operated, repairing a broken pelvic bone.

Bridle didn't like the hospital and begged constantly to go home. She was moved to a nursing home near Branson, and later to one in Ava nearer her home. She was sitting in a wheelchair reading a large-print *Reader's Digest* when I visited her. She wanted to know about home – had I been to her cabin; was it OK? She said she was going home just as soon as they would let her. I mentioned how very impressed the young *USA Today* reporter was when he visited her three years earlier, how he was struck because she was unaware of the Beatles and Elvis Presley. She smiled and said, "Yes, he was a nice young man and was especially baffled that I didn't know those people – I guess they were singers, weren't they?" I told her they were; then she said, "I thought it was funny that he had never heard of Barnabas."

Less than nine months after leaving her cabin in the woods on that New Year's Day, Birdle Mannon died in the Heart of the Ozarks Nursing Home in Ava and is buried with her family near the little log house where she lived for eighty-three years.

While cleaning out her cabin, we found, among many other things, two homemade suitcases in the attic. Inside were beautiful paintings by Samuel Mannon, some dated in the late 1800s; letters; photographs; and checkbooks. We gave all the findings to Southwest Missouri State University, which Birdle attended in 1939 and 1940. They are now preserved in the SMSU library's Ozarks History section and often displayed for public viewing.

In February 2003, Silver Dollar City near Branson carefully dismantled Birdle's cabin and removed it to the theme park, where two million visitors a year are able to view and enjoy the home of a true pioneer woman. In collaboration with the university, Silver Dollar City will display replicas of Samuel's paintings, photographs of Birdle and her family, letters more than a hundred years old, a rusty well pump and even the outhouse, handmade by Samuel Mannon.

PHOTOS BY LEE ANN RUSSELL

Birdle Mannon lived in this little cabin eighty-three of her ninety years. It is now displayed, along with her family memorabilia, at Silver Dollar City near Branson, Missouri.

This old wood-burning stove cooked all Birdle's meals.

PART II

By Brothers Jim and Sim Evans

From left, front, are Sim and Jim Evans. In back are their sister Barbara and brother Wayne.

The Evans brothers grew up on a farm near Bradleyville but nearer the McClurg, Missouri post office.

Jim decided not to finish high school at Bradleyville and left, hitchhiking to greener pastures in California when he was seventeen. He worked there a while, served a hitch in the U. S. Air Force, and then enjoyed a successful career with IBM in Southern California where he and his wife lived in retirement until their recent move to Georgia to be nearer children and grandchildren.

Sim Evans didn't wait to drop out of school. He and Dean Lewis ran away from home when they were about sixteen and headed for the faraway state of next-door Kansas. When he settled down and after a stint in the U. S. Army, Sim completed a highly rewarding career with National Cash Register Corporation. He and his wife now live retired near Dayton, Ohio.

19

THE OZARK MOUNTAINS

By Sim Evans

It is always risky to listen to stories from strangers, so we need to get to know each other. You can never really know a man until you know where he's from, for a man becomes himself early on, and then he is shaped by his family and by his homeland. That is why in the olden days, if you wanted to know about a man, you began by asking about where he was from. Occasionally you hear this question asked even today. So I'll start by telling you about myself and my homeland and a little about my family.

I came from the Ozarks. This land of my childhood was a beautiful place; a vast mountainous and hilly land, made early on in creation and not yet spoiled by the works of man. It once was and is no more. Some say it never really existed, but I know better because I was there.

I was born in a log cabin on a hillside, deep in the Ozarks. The cabin was built sometime in the nineteenth century and had once been substantial enough to deserve being called a house. There once were two, possibly even three, rooms, with a loft, a hallway, and porches, front and back, and a fireplace, built of large rectangular cut stones. God only knows where they came from. But by the time of my earliest memories, the years had taken their toll on the cabin. The chimney and the north room had deteriorated to the point of becoming dangerous and so had to come down. The hallway was boarded over and became a kitchen, and the back porch was covered so as to become a bedroom.

"Let me tell you a story of the land of my youth, the Ozark Hills. The story happened long ago, and I am very old now so I must tell it before I grow too forgetful."

This bedroom never knew heat. It was well ventilated, as the south wall was of simple boards, unpainted and withered. With the passage of time they shrunk, leaving cracks through which the sunlight and the moonlight and the snow and the rain all passed during their allotted season. My father told me he had heard from old men that sleeping in a room with heat was unhealthy; so even then, I already had a leg up on the world. I was blessed at an early age. I can see this clearly now.

The forest grew close-in. It was a strange mixture of the old, the new, and the second-growth. The land was thin and poor, and domesticated crops of any kind could only be grown with difficulty. On the other hand, the indigenous plant life was so marvelously adapted to the soil and climate they grew with an unquenchable ferocity. One could cleanse a field of persimmon and sassafras bushes twenty years running all to no avail; miss two years and the field became a sea of brush. Hand tools were insufficient to stave off the onslaught. Nature had her foot planted firmly in the small of man's back, and it seemed it would ever be so.

At night the screech owls would come right up to the trees in the yard and emit their eerie, humanlike screams. In the background the hoot owls would periodically emit their deep, mournful hoots, first from one direction then another. The whippoorwills were everywhere, literally filling the night with sound. There were hound dogs, big ones and little ones. On clear nights the little ones would spy the moon and, sometimes forgetting they had been domesticated for ten thousand years, sit on their haunches and give forth the primitive howl of their ancestors. This would awaken the selfsame instinct within the other dogs, and before long the moon was being serenaded as was the custom in the olden days. Dogs seldom howl anymore, and I miss it. Progress seems to have stifled their imaginations.

And the bats! They would come out at dusk by the tens of thousands, sometimes thick enough to block out the moon. In quest of sustenance they would swoop close to the ground, and many times I felt the swipe of a bat wing on my head. All this was fearsome and exciting to me as a child, and I must admit the fearsome part sometimes got the better of me and I would not venture far from the cabin door.

Far up those dark old hollows lived old men who could stop the flow of blood from a wound by simply laying their hands on the wounded and old women who could remove warts. There were haunted houses and even haunted caves. It was rumored that a neighbor boy, having gone in a haunted cave, had come upon the jawbone of an old cow. When he picked it up and wiggled it at the hinge, it said, "Quit!" I never went in that cave.

There were marvelous storytellers in the Ozarks back then. I learned much about how things were in the old days and more about how they should have been. And ghost stories! When Ethel Davidson told a ghost story, you didn't walk home by yourself.

My maternal grandfather waited until he was older to raise a family, so he was very old even when I was small. When he was young, he sat at the feet of Civil War veterans who were yet healing, so he had stories that were captivating to a child. He once walked to Texas, and he spent much time in the Indian Territories. He could whoop like an Indian and never tired of telling me about the "Territory." My grandmother served as editor and sometimes had to correct his stories, but I am satisfied that, in the main, they were the gospel. One thing bothers me; history tells us that in those days, the Indian territories were mainly populated by bad men who were often on the run from the law. I worry about this.

Both Grandma and Grandpa were products of the Civil War. They were the baby boomers of that era. As such, they were reared by men and women who had just gone through the most awful ordeal since Cromwell. I have studied much history, but little is written about the effect of the war on the Ozarks. Two major battles are mentioned, and historians speak in generalities about the "disorganized nature of the fighting."

But the old folks told a much more understandable story. As a child I heard stories that literally made the hair stand up on the back of my neck. Stories about an old couple being forcibly removed from their humble dwelling in preparation for the burning. And when the family Bible was discovered in the old lady's skirts, it was taken away and thrown onto the fire. To fully understand this, you need to know that the family Bible contained all written records of that civilization. The weddings, the births, and the deaths – all were recorded there. And tucked away somewhere in the pages you would likely find a lock of hair from a beloved infant who died long ago and maybe a withered flower from his grave.

I was told how the Federals would come and build sawmills and then command that all able-bodied men should work there. If they refused, they were shot. If they worked, the Rebel "irregulars" would come and shoot them and their families in the dark of night and burn everything for good measure. It is a fact of history that in wars, those who live in the debatable lands drink from a bitter cup. A civilization was being destroyed.

The aftermath was worse. The country was filled with desperadoes who had long since despaired of God, country, and their fellow man; they were truly deserving of the name outlaw. They were deemed unworthy of due process and could be shot on sight. These were desperate men.

Through it all, some persevered; having no civilization, they took their double-bitted axes and their rifles and built anew. This new civilization was a paintless one, and it had sharp edges; it was inhabited by hard men. It was a make-do civilization. They spoke a language that was similar to Middle English and clung to their traditions with an uncommon tenacity, and their traditions were so old they seemed to have seeped from the soil.

These people had firsthand knowledge of the ham-fisted nature of government. They had been visited by brutality and atrocities from both Yankee and Rebel and had seen unspeakable acts committed by neighbor against neighbor in the name of partisanship. They had felt the hot breath of chaos and anarchy, and they had had enough. They hated and feared all government and all things strange, and they mistrusted their neighbors. Prior allegiances and political leanings were seldom spoken of, and much verbal history was lost. Within a few short generations the people knew not from whence they came; nothing was written, and the past was spoken about in whispers. Such a void had not been seen since the Dark Ages.

The people were taciturn, suspicious, and secretive, and they turned inward on themselves. And they were isolated, as there was no coal or iron or oil to bring new people and new ideas. This isolation was heightened by the people's distrust of all things government, and it did the inevitable; it crystallized the civilization. Progress rolled around those hills on the north and the south and left them much unchanged for almost one hundred years. It was from these seeds that I sprang.

My grandpa's house was a small, one-room log affair. The roof was covered with rusty tin and was steep. The pitch abruptly lessened over both the front and back porches. The back porch was completely walled-in and served as the kitchen. Here was the cook stove, fired with wood. There was always a teakettle sitting on the stove, with a marble inside to collect the excess lime. Ever-present on the kitchen table were jelly, bread, and homemade butter, along with sugar, salt and pepper, pepper sauce, cold cornbread and other good things. These were covered with a large cloth when not in use; this kept away the flies.

The main room contained a wood heating stove, a dresser, a rocking chair by the window, and the bed where Grandpa slept and died. Upstairs in the loft I could go and play with my great-granddad's crutch, for he only had one leg, and his old muzzle-loading rifle. I'm told my great-granddad used to kill bear with that old muzzleloader propped up in the fork of a stick. We didn't have any bears when I was a child; I was sorry about this, because I wanted to kill one.

Half the front porch was completely boxed in and was known as the "side room." This was where my Aunt Lenora slept when she came all the way from Portland to visit during WW II. On the outside walls climbed the ever-present gourds and morning glories.

One morning I came to visit my grandpa, and he was sitting on this half-sized front porch. He was smoking his pipe and fondling a giant forty-four-caliber revolver. He would carefully turn the cylinder, observing each of those big bullets as they rolled around. Then he would cock the hammer and let it down, all the time watching the road.

Grandma and Grandpa always treated me as an adult and would tell me everything, so I soon learned Grandpa was expecting a gentleman caller – a man with whom he had fought many, many years ago. Grandma informed me that Grandpa had cut this gentleman's throat. Grandpa readily admitted this. He also confessed to me that, through a combination of carelessness and haste, he had botched the job, leaving the gentleman with a lifelong scar on his throat as a constant reminder. "But," said Grandpa, gently waving the barrel of his ancient revolver, "if he shows up, I'll get 'er right this time." The gentleman never showed, and peace reigned in my small world.

Wild grapes in those hills were as delicious as any domestic grape you ever ate, and they grew high in the trees so you had to climb to get them. In the fall they were plentiful, and you could eat some while walking to school and some on the way home. There were wild strawberries in the spring, of course, and in summer, gooseberries gone wild.

The cold, freshwater springs in those hills had water as good as you could ever want.

The coldest and the best was in the Huffman cave. I used to go there by myself as a child. I would take a gun and a knife and go off creepy-silent into the woods and walk the five miles or so to the cave. The cave went far back into the mountain and turned to the right, so it soon became pitch black. This darkness required a torch, made of dead sticks and lit with a kitchen match. Finally, when you reached the back of the cave, you found the coolest, clearest water in the world. It ran out of the mountainside, and lay in a big pool at your feet. Overhead was a big sandstone dome, and in the firelight it looked just like gold. I used to pretend that it was and that I alone knew where it was. You can't go to the Huffman cave anymore. The government has placed iron bars at the front so none can enter. Maybe government officials thought someone would steal the water. Whatever the reason, a generation of children is poorer for this foolishness.

On the way, there were squirrels to hunt, and crows and an occasional hawk to shoot. Now I am aware that it is politically incorrect to shoot hawks today, but we were taught to shoot hawks because they were death on chickens. Nobody shoots hawks anymore because nobody has chickens. If the hawks ate your chickens and made you hungry, you'd shoot them too. I tried eating a hawk once. Chickens are better.

Some years the squirrels were plentiful (we ate 'em) and some years scarce as hen's teeth. All years they were wild. When you see the squirrels in the city park, it's hard to imagine how wild they can get. But just go down to the park and kill a few and eat them and you'll see. I know they are cuddly warm little things, but it is good you understand that when people are hungry they will eat cuddly, warm little things. In the final extremity, before they starve, people will even eat you, so be prepared.

I'll tell you a few things about hunting squirrels, just in case you're ever real hungry but not yet ready to eat your little brother. The best way is without dogs, because you can find them better than a dog if you are serious about your business. You must move through the woods very slowly and silently, like a shadow, and occasionally spend long periods of time absolutely motionless. It's called "still hunting." Just keep your eyes peeled. The human brain is marvelously adept at pattern recognition, and soon you'll be able to tell the difference between a stick or a leaf or a clump and part of a squirrel. Now here is the secret: A squirrel always knows where he is and where his tail is, but he always forgets his ears and leaves them sticking out in plain sight. Don't ask me why. So when you are good enough to spot a squirrel's ear sticking out from behind a hickory tree at fifty yards, here's what you do: Take careful aim at the ear, but before you shoot, pull slightly inward, just enough to cut the bark. That way you'll get him for sure. It's called "barking the tree." My father taught me to do this before I was six years old. I thought it was pretty neat, and I ate a lot more often because of it.

There were no dragons in the Ozarks, but we had plenty of stuff to worry about without dragons. Of course we had scarlet fever and infantile paralysis, like the rest of the world, but you either caught it and died or you didn't; nobody worried about it. We had stuff that was worse: chiggers. Chiggers are not peculiar to the Ozarks, but we nearly cornered the market. Chiggers are little red critters, so small they are invisible to all but children with exceptional eyesight. Many people have been bitten repeatedly by these little devils, yet gone to their graves never having seen one. Pound for pound, they have a worse bite than a great white shark. In addition, they inject an itching compound, which drives you crazy. My father told me a secret about this after I had suffered much. If you don't scratch a chigger bite it will go away after about twenty-four hours. If you do, it will last maybe six weeks, fester up, and cause you no end of grief. Nothing is for sure in this world, but it worked for me.

We had wood ticks. They came in three sizes: dog ticks (big), yearlings (medium-sized), and seed ticks (small). Seed ticks, like all things small, came in great bunches and would spread out over your whole body in no time at all. Sometimes it would take weeks to ferret them all out. The only antidote we ever found was a product called Black Leaf Forty. It was a by-product of tobacco and boy was it good! It would kill anything: chiggers, ticks, even maybe a small calf! Alas, this product was soon outlawed and taken off the market. I believe the people in town, not having any ticks or chiggers, did this for spite.

Snakes were plentiful in this land. We had copperheads everywhere; in the spring-house, in the grass, in the henhouse and in our house. It was always best to check under your pillow before going to bed. My father helped me identify the smell of a copperhead when he is riled, and that may have saved me, because I've never been bitten. But this may also be attributed to my hatred for snakes, a strange and unreasoned hate: primitive and deadly. When I was a child all my friends hated snakes. We were constantly on the lookout, and if we encountered a snake, we killed it; poisonous or not, it didn't matter. It was better having one of us around than having a good snake dog. Someday when I go to the zoo, I just might fill my pockets with rocks and kill all their snakes.

Only one of my friends, a Dunn, was ever bitten. One of those Dunn kids sat down beside a log and was bitten by a rattlesnake. I don't believe it would have hurt him all that much, because he was a tough kid. But his father cut an X with his knife, so he could suck the venom out, and the poor boy will carry the scar all his life, I fear. These Dunn boys were my friends, and I sometimes stayed overnight with them after school, but I have forgotten their first names. (Their sister's name was Charlotte; I remember that because she was very pretty. I bet she still is.)

Farther afield we had a few ground rattlers and cottonmouths aplenty. For a child, the cottonmouths were the most to be feared, for they were the most poisonous. In addition, they were aggressive, and would chase you down and bite you, and when you fell over, if they were hungry, they would try to eat you. They were just plain mean.

Countless varieties of nonpoisonous snakes existed. Chief among these were black snakes as long as a fence rail and coachwhips big enough to swallow a dog. And then there was the bane of all children, the blue racer, a longish, harmless snake, whose main line of defense was to charge! Right at you. If you retreated, he would continue to advance. If you charged back, he would retreat as prudence dictated. I was put to flight many times by these little devils before I found the courage to stand my ground. I find much that is admirable about these little blue snakes.

There were other kinds of snakes in this land I am speaking of, strange and exotic snakes. We never saw them but we knew they were there, for we were told about them. There was the hoop snake: He had a hook on the end of his tail, and if he spied you when he was on the uphill side, he would place this hook in the corner of his mouth, form himself into a hoop, or wheel, and roll down the hill and get you. As I understood it, this was a very fast snake indeed once he got rolling. Worse yet was the joint snake. You couldn't kill it. You could smash away with rocks until you were blue in the face, and you still couldn't kill it. You see, upon being struck, it would break into a thousand little joints, then come sundown, it would put itself back together and track you down while you were in bed, sound asleep. My grandfather told me all about these snakes when I was very young, and for years I always kept a sharp lookout. I never saw any, so I guess they must keep pretty much to themselves. But they're there.

There was no money in this land I knew as a child, for God built the Ozarks first and for its beauty alone. I think he built it for us kids. Beneath its beauty was a hard land, but how else were we going to grow strong and resourceful? Besides, we were the lords of creation. It was all ours, as far as the naked eye could see and bare feet could walk. And we had neither the means nor the inclination to hurt the land.

Across all the years I still have a special memory that ranks above the others. In this memory I am eight years old and on the way home from Grandpa's house. I come down this little lane that breaks out into an open field dotted with persimmon and black walnut trees. This would be just after I cross the cattle guard. The milk cows are all here, grazing peacefully, and they are my friends. There is old Crazy-Cow, whom I stay away from, and old Red, who gives the sweetest milk. And old Brownie, who claimed me as her own and would allow me to get a drink of milk any time I wanted it. And when I would bend down to squirt the milk in my mouth, she would bless me with a rake of her sandpapery tongue across my bare back. Please don't look down on this, because the milk was warm and sweet, and on a cold frosty morning it goes rather well with ripe persimmons.

A fall nip fills the air, offset by the warm, late-afternoon sun. The deep dust, turned to powder, has accumulated heat throughout the day and feels warm and cozy to a boy's bare feet. This is how it is in mid-October, when Indian Summer is at its best. To my left I can see the mountain crest, as it runs west. The leaves have turned colors of which I have yet to learn the names. In front of me, the hills in their resplendent colors roll on and on until they finally become blue and turn upward at a tangent and meet the sky. To my right is Grandpa's old orchard, where a few peach trees still survive and are worth visiting. Down the lane I can see home. It's just an old cabin with a tin roof, but I can see smoke coming out the stovepipe, and I know there are beans on the stove. And I know there is a safe place close by when dark drives me home.

As the sun slid down toward the hills, it became bigger and bigger, until it was as big as a washtub and blood red. Then God opened a young child's mind, and I heard an inner voice say, You may go far away and do many things, but you will never see such beauty or know a place so peaceful as this, your Ozark home. And so it has been.

Later that evening I discussed this with my mother. I told her about the trees with all their splendid colors and how they were so beautiful, but she was not impressed. She said, "Son, you don't understand. Them trees are dressing up for their own funeral." I guess women like the springtime better.

And now I sense that you have become rather comfortable with me, and I'll bet you're just dying to ask me questions. Am I right? And I'll bet the big question in your mind is this: What ever happened to these old Ozark hills of your childhood days? Why are they no more as they once were? Well, I'll cut through all the fuzzy stuff and get right to the hard truth. Electricity came and ruined it all.

20

THE LAST
PUBLIC HANGING IN AMERICA

By Sim Evans

Often I speak of the peace and tranquillity of my childhood days in the Ozark Mountains and how the young people were moderately well behaved and didn't go round tearing the clothes off young women.

And even when the local basketball team won the state championship, they didn't burn cars, break windows and riot. And just as often, people speculate as to why this was so. Just the other day I mentioned this phenomenon to an old friend, and he said, "Yeah, I know, but those were gentler times." I refrained from telling him, but this was not so.

My ancestors settled in a remote area of the Ozarks in the 1820s. They came from Virginia and North Carolina and Kentucky, and they were the have-nots, the scoundrels, the adventurers, the landless and the loners. They passed over the Bootheel delta land of Missouri, possibly the most fertile farmland in the world, and instead settled in those barren and rocky hills that comprise some of the oldest mountains in the world, the Ozark Mountains. Such is the lot of the mountain man, for he is irresistibly drawn to where the earth tilts upward.

Scarcely had a generation passed when the Civil War was upon them. They found themselves in the debatable land, where neither the North nor the South could prevail; thus they were ground between the upper and the nether stones of the Union and Confederate governments.

The aftermath was almost as bad as the war. Bad men with bounties on their heads came to that remote area and proceeded to take what little there was of value at the point of a gun. Vigilante committees were formed, and the outlaws were hanged. But no sooner was this accomplished than the vigilantes turned on the general populace and became hooded tyrants, spreading terror in the night.

Then sheriffs were elected with explicit instructions to hang the vigilantes. This they proceeded to do with gusto. Finally in the late 1880s, the last of the vigilantes were caught and hanged. Out of all this came a generation of men, born around the turn of the twentieth century, who were hard and bitter – and mean. If you took issue with them, they would fight at the drop of a hat, and they would give no warning. The old traditions and the old law prevailed: an eye for an eye and a tooth for a tooth.

If new laws were passed that were not consistent with the old traditions, they were ignored. And if government officials wished to push an issue, jury nullification was the answer they got; they got it often. There were certain things you just didn't do: You didn't use foul language around women, you didn't kill people, you didn't steal, and you didn't fail to pay your debts. In fact, if you insisted on making a nuisance of yourself, you didn't last too long. If a young man got in a bar fight, those old men would observe the bruises and laugh at him. If he went down to the country store and started a fight, they might hurt him. There was a time and a place for everything.

At length, public virtue was established and eventually became interwoven with the prevailing culture. For a time the old men could afford to walk softly. Then two major upheavals occurred almost simultaneously: one of a revolutionary nature and the other cataclysmic. The former was the general availability of the automobile, which allowed the more adventuresome to escape their immediate environs and attain a certain degree of anonymity. This alone was the cause of a great deal of mischief. The latter was the Great Depression, which spawned mini-migrations to the north and west.

Which brings me to the last public hanging in America.

Roscoe Jackson was a young man from the Ozarks. He was but a youth, having a pleasing countenance and flaming red hair. He was commonly known as 'Red' Jackson. Being adventuresome, he left his native land and made his way to Oklahoma to seek his fortune in the then-fledgling oil fields. While there he kept questionable company, learned bad ways, and forgot the teachings of his childhood.

Time passed, his dreams did not materialize, and home called. Like so many other youths of that time, he began the long trek home using his thumb. He nearly made it. In August 1934, within ten miles of home, he decided to rob and kill the man who had given him a ride on the last leg of his journey.

The deed done, Roscoe stashed the unfortunate victim's body in the remote woods and removed eighteen dollars from the man's pocket. Then, using the victim's car, rushed back to Oklahoma, whence he had just come.

Within three days the victim had been identified, and Red Jackson's complicity ascertained from eyewitnesses. The victim's son, being a man of means, took the county sheriff and, at his own expense, went to Oklahoma and hunted young Jackson down. The son and the sheriff brought him back to the Ozarks and locked him away in jail.

He immediately escaped. After a 45-day manhunt, he was again run to ground and again incarcerated, this time with heavy guard. There were to be no more escapes.

On May 21, 1937, less than three years after the terrible deed, Roscoe Jackson took his last walk. He climbed the fourteen steps of the gallows in Galena, Missouri, and turned to face the crowd. Here were the curious and the concerned, the children who came to see electric lights for the first time and eat ice cream and the old men who came to see him die.

Roscoe gazed at the crowd and said, "Well now, folks, it ain't everybody that knows what it takes to die. It's easy when it comes accidental, but it's not so easy when it comes gradual." Then the black hood was slipped over his head as he spoke his last words, "Well, be good, folks." Then Sheriff Coin pulled the lever, and Red Jackson plunged to his death.

Thus ended the last public hanging in the United States of America, in the little town of Galena, Missouri, which is situated in Stone County. And thus began thirty years of peace and public tranquility the likes of which you have never seen. And even today a young lady can walk unattended from one end of the county to the other and not likely be harmed.

Such were the power and character of those hard, old men and their homemade laws.

People hear me tell this, and they say, "What are we to make of all this?" And I reply, "Make of it what you want." Then they say, "Well, what do you make of it?" And I say, "Nothing; I just tell the story as it happened."

Then they just smile, shake their heads and go away.

But just between you and me, I do make something of it: It occurs to me that nowadays when lawlessness abounds and our young have run amok, a bunch of mothers always get together and protest. They leave their children at home, fly to Washington, and call their mission a "Million Mom March" or something similar. Once there, they plead with the government to protect them and their children. Discounting the mischief their children get into while they are gone, not much ever comes of these affairs.

In the old days it was different. When heinous crimes were committed, a few hard, old men would hang the offender. They would do it quickly and in broad daylight. They would do it legally, under the full color of authority, and they would encourage you to come and see, and bring the children. And they would advertise sufficiently to draw a good crowd.

And strangely enough, when this happened an amazing tranquility would fall over the community and sometimes last for a long generation.

Now I would never advocate a return to this type of justice, for we are too compassionate and too enlightened and too civilized for that.

But just between you and me, do you have a better idea?

21

DAD DISCOVERS ELECTRICITY

BY JIM EVANS

Jim Evans went to a one-room school for grades one through eight.

Growing up on a small farm in the hills of southern Missouri, one lesson my brothers and I learned early in life was to obey our parents' orders or instructions without argument and with very few questions. Not only that, we learned never to sass or show disrespect toward other adults in the community. Like most parents of that era and region, they believed in corporal punishment and would not hesitate to practice it. When we started our first day of school, our mother warned us as we left the house to "mind the teacher." Often we were promised that if we were punished or "got a whipping" at school, we would receive even more punishment when we got home.

Like most boys in the one-room schools that were taught mostly by girls seventeen to twenty years of age, I got my share of whippings. Fortunately for me, my parents never learned of most of them. Often the only effective way a teacher could maintain discipline of the rowdy country boys of those days was to whip all the boys in sight whenever any one of them started to become unruly. Because almost all the mischief was done by boys, the girls didn't get many whippings, especially if they turned us in.

Once, when she was unable to identify who threw a rock at a passing car, the teacher, Miss Arlee Dann, whipped all the boys she could find. My friend Billy Potter and I had gone home for lunch and were not present when the incident occurred; however, because the girls pointed a finger at us, we both were punished anyway. We spent the next several recess periods talking about how we would get even with the girls. We decided to make a miniature sling shot and shoot their backsides with BB pellets. It worked very well at first – they thought they were being stung by bees. In fact, it worked so well that we tried it on the teacher. Of course that proved to be a major mistake on our part, because it didn't take long for her to figure out it was Billy and me. The punishment we received for that ill-advised stunt served as an example to all other students of what she was willing to do if pressed. From that day on, the entire student body was a much better behaved group. For several days, Billy and I were the best behaved boys in the entire school.

Most of the whippings I received were not really severe at all, at least the ones given by my mother and the younger schoolteachers. I quickly learned that the older, more experienced teachers whipped harder and therefore adjusted my behavior accordingly. A whipping by my dad was another matter. He seldom actually whipped us, but on the rare occasions when he did it was usually severe enough that we didn't forget it quickly. A mere scolding by him was worse than a whipping from my mother; just the thought of getting a whipping by him was enough to keep me on my toes most of the time. Even though he was sometimes a harsh disciplinarian, he was not totally without a sense of fairness or a good sense of humor.

Perhaps I deserved some of the whippings he gave me but by no means all of them, one in particular that neither of us forgot.

One morning when I was about ten or eleven years old, my dad instructed me to check on a litter of newborn pigs on my way to school. I did as he instructed and found that the pigs were dead. Of course there was nothing anyone could do about it at that time, so I just continued on my way to school. Later in the day he checked on them himself, and finding them dead, he mistakenly thought that I had not cared for them properly. For punishment he gave me a few vigorous whacks with the reins of a horse bridle; I felt it, even through my baggy overalls. Later that evening I was able to convince him that it was not my fault that the pigs had died.

The next morning he and I went out to make the daily check of a battery powered-electric fence that we had ordered from the Montgomery Ward catalog and installed to keep our livestock from a small field of oats. I was following several yards behind him as we walked through the oats and grass that were still wet from an early-morning rain and of course our shoes, pants legs and feet were soaking wet. Electricity had not yet reached our community so we had little knowledge of it. I knew from an article that I had read in a magazine, however, that the water on our shoes and the wet ground made us excellent conductors of electricity. I also knew that my father had a phobia concerning electricity, probably because he didn't know how it worked or why it would shock you. I was still angry because he had not yet apologized for the unwarranted whipping he had given me the previous day. As we walked along checking the fence, I thought of a way to get my revenge.

When we reached a spot in the field where the water from the rain was still about an inch or more in depth and I could see my father's feet nearly submerged in the water and mud, I knew the time was right. Keeping a safe distance between us, I held my hand very near the electric-fence wire while really not touching it. I called out to him, "Hey, Dad, something is wrong with this fence; it has no juice in it." As I had hoped, he looked at my hand that only appeared to be grasping the wire and fell for my trick and grabbed the fence himself. Being as wet as he was, he did indeed make an excellent conductor; with each pulse of the electric fence he would jump and shout, but he was unable to get loose from the fence. After a dozen or more pulses, each one successively causing him to shout louder and jerk more violently, he managed to free himself. Of course he immediately expressed some level of anger toward me. I don't recall the exact words he used, but in effect he said, "You'd better have a damn good reason for deliberately doing something this foolish. That hurts!" He started cutting a branch from an elm tree and obviously intended to whip me with it. Seeing this, I quickly scooted under the electric fence to put a little more distance between us. Before he finished making the branch ready, I said "Well, that whipping yesterday wasn't exactly fair ..." He muttered something unintelligible under his breath, and his anger vanished immediately as he turned and continued walking down the fence row, keeping several feet of distance between himself and the wire. "That kind of foolishness could kill someone," he finally said.

Thirty-five years later, while visiting him in the hospital where he had just had a heart control pacemaker installed in his chest, I asked him if it would be necessary to adjust it periodically. He laughed and said, "Oh, if it slows down I'll just grab on to an electric fence to speed it up some."

22

COFFEE CANS
ARE THE KEY TO SURVIVAL

By Sim Evans

Things were different back in forty-nine. Some say times were simpler back then, but that's not really true. Not unless being perpetually in the survival mode is simpler than walking up and down the mall in sloppy pants and purple hair. Some say we held things together back then with bailing wire and spit, but that's not true either. Coffee cans saved the day.

In those days our diet was mostly meat, and we had to kill everything we ate. I have heard people say that when young people kill animals, it causes them to become serial killers when they grow up, but I'm not too sure about that. My brother-in-law, Lester, always killed his own food. He fought all through the war, then worked for a big meat

Sim Evans, left, and his brother Jim led an exciting childhood in the hills of Southwest Missouri.

packing plant for twenty years after that; and he was a real nice guy. Of course if you got smart with him he would bust you one real quick. But then his whole bunch was like that.

I can recall, as if but yesterday, those frosty mornings when Dad would say, "Son, get a coffee can full of coal-oil and start a fire, while I shoot a hog." After I started the fire, and Dad shot the hog, we would hoist him up by his hind legs and I would cut his throat with a butcher knife. Now don't cringe, because this is the generally accepted procedure, and recommended by the USDA. In fact, the USDA insists it be done this way. Besides, I tell you these gruesome things for a reason. Everyone has heard on occasion the descriptive term, "He bled like a stuck pig." Now you understand the origin of the phrase.

Scraping the hair off the hog is the tricky part. To do this you must heat water, throw it on the hog, then scrape like mad before it cools off. Here again we use the coffee can. The temperature of the water is crucial. If it is too cold, the hair won't scrape off, and you have to do it all over again. And if it is too hot, it will set the hair permanently, and you can't ever scrape it off. This phenomenon is called 'setting the hair,' and if it happens you have to skin the hog. Nobody likes to skin a hog.

So now when you hear some old man say that something is "Hot enough to set the hair on a hog," you'll know what it means. It means something got too hot.

The usefulness of a coffee can was practically unlimited in those days. The amount of feed the livestock received each day was not measured in grams or pounds, but by the number of coffee cans. If the stove pipe developed a hole, you split a coffee can and slipped it around the pipe. And when you took a bath in the spring branch, it was with the ubiquitous coffee can that you reached upstream to get clear water to dump on yourself.

You may think this is all about the past and of no use to you, but you'd better watch out. Just last month, as my birthday rolled around, I realized my old pickup was due for license inspection. Now you know how the government is about inspection: They can't catch old Bin Laden, and they haven't a clue who sent the anthrax germs to all those people; but if you mess with their license inspection program, they will have you under house arrest in an instant.

So it was with some trepidation that I viewed the state of the muffler on my old pickup. It was full of holes. With the aid of a few coffee cans and coat hanger wire, I had it patched up in no time, and it sailed right through inspection. Just perfect. What was true in the old days is still true today. You can't survive without coffee cans.

23

WHY I'M AFRAID OF SNAKES

BY JIM EVANS

For as long as I can remember I have had a deathly fear of snakes, even harmless grass snakes. My children discovered my fear when they were very young and had much fun, at my expense, playing little tricks on me. Once my daughter brought home a pet snake belonging to her friend and placed it around my neck while I was sleeping. She then woke me, yelling, "Dad there's a snake in your bed." To her, and the others' delight, I panicked and ran from the house in my pajamas.

Of course that was great entertainment for the kids; they have told and retold that story many times, to everyone we know. My daughter even wrote an essay for one of her classes about "the time we put a snake in Dad's bed." Of course they think my fear is foolish and they're probably correct. Foolish or not I can live with it.

When I was a small boy, the farmhouse I grew up in had been abandoned for many years before my parents moved into it during the midst of the depression in 1934, a few days before I was born. The surrounding grounds were overgrown with brush and weeds. In addition to that, there were several dilapidated old storage buildings filled with odds and ends left by the last people who had lived there nearly 30 years before. This environment made an ideal location for the poisonous copperhead snakes. Soon after my parents moved in they discovered a copperhead den nearby; they destroyed the den quickly but it took several years to completely rid our house and the surrounding grounds of them. My mother kept a count and said that during the first five years they killed more than fifty copperheads in and near the house. Consequentially, I and my brothers and sisters learned at a young age to be cautious when walking in an area that might be a good habitat for snakes. We learned, for example, to peek under our beds in the morning before stepping down with our bare feet because several times we found a snake that had crawled under the bed during the night. I still am cautious even in areas where there are no snakes.

One of the snake killings I remember happened when I was about four years old. My dad, mother and brother Wayne were working in the fields. My sister Barbara who was 11 years old was assigned to prepare the noon meal for them and watch over me. In our yard was an old wood frame building that had once been a general store, operated by my great-grandparents in the late 1800s, but had been abandoned for many years and was pretty much falling down. Inside it were pieces of old harness and a couple of old saddles, an old yarn spinning wheel and other old junk from the long ago, just the sort of place a curious four-year-old boy would be attracted to.

My mom had warned me not to play in the old building because of the danger of snakes and the possibility that the dilapidated old building would fall on me. However, while my sister was busy preparing lunch, I entered the old building anyway. I was crawling under some old boards when I spotted a copperhead coiled about 12 inches from my face. I quickly scrambled out and went for my big sister. She took my dad's .22-caliber repeating rifle (a Marlin lever action holding 17 rounds in the magazine) and shot the snake from a range of about 6 feet; the snake still moved so she shot it again; it still moved so she kept shooting until the gun was empty. But the snake was still twisting and squirming and attempting to bite anything near it.

Not knowing what else to do at that time we thought it would be a good idea to call our parents; we stuck a pitchfork in the snake to pin it to the ground so he couldn't crawl away. We had a large hunter's horn – a bullhorn fitted with a mouth piece, normally used by our father to call his dogs from long distances. With practice one could sound it so that it would be heard for several miles.

The horn was also used to signal various messages; we often used it as a dinner bell by blowing a series of short blasts, or toots, which signaled those who were working in the fields that lunch was ready. All the children had been taught to blow that old horn loudly and in long blasts if we had an emergency when no adults were present. On this occasion my sister blew as loudly and as long as she could and naturally my parents recognizing that we had an emergency came quickly.

Dad was plowing with a horse drawn plow when he first heard the alarm. He quickly unhitched the horse and jumped on without removing the harness. I still remember him galloping the horse, "Old Topsy," into the front yard with the harness and traces flapping wildly.

The snake was badly wounded but still alive and able to strike and bite. Dad cut off its head with a shovel and said that it appeared all the 17 shots my sister had fired hit the snake. He complimented us several times for remaining calm and said we handled the situation properly.

Although I remember finding and killing many snakes in the years that followed, that was the most memorable. In fact that snake coiled a few inches from my face is the most vivid memory of my childhood. I was nearly a grown man before we eventually eradicated all the copperheads within a half mile of our house but I never lost my fear. Even today, more than sixty years later, whenever I see a movie scene depicting someone handling snakes, my heart starts pounding and I feel like I'm going to throw up. I can actually taste the same fear that I felt that day.

24

THE SNITCH HUNT

BY SIM EVANS

I f you've ever been to school, then you know this: there are snitches everywhere. They sit in the classrooms as calm as you please and act just like ordinary people. They hide in the bathroom stalls and listen to everything you say. They ride the school buses and inhabit the cafeteria. And the minute you do or say something wrong, they tell on you. They make you miserable.

Now, they can't help this, for they are like aliens who can make themselves look like us. They probably want to be like us, but they can't. You see, ordinary food does them no good. They feed on snitching. They must get in one good snitch every day before the sun goes down, or they just wither away and disappear. So you can see why they work so very hard.

They are dangerous; make no mistake about that. They are wolves in sheep's clothing. The trick is to jerk away their sheepy cover and make them show their fangs. That way, when a snitch approaches a herd of ordinary boys and girls, they can scatter. This confuses the snitch, for he is none too bright, and chances are he'll go sit in the classroom alone. That way, you can soon get back to the really important things in life, like tearing the net off the basketball hoop.

Now the school I attended was small, with probably no more than one hundred students, top to bottom. In addition, if the truth be told, most of us were related to one another, in many cases more than once. If this confuses you, I am sorry, but I'm not going to go into it further. The next time you hear someone refer to their double cousin twice removed, you just dig into it yourself, and then you'll know what I mean.

We all knew one another, and for the most part, we constantly talked about one another's activities or "doings," as we referred to them back then. I'm sure you know the kind of harmless, childish stuff I am talking about, like who had gone fishing with dynamite most recently, or who had jumped off the Old Beaver bridge and lived to tell the tale. Add to this the exchange of technical information, such as how to skip school and avoid detection, the best way to spotlight deer and avoid game wardens, or how to get one-up on the enterprising citizens who encased their mailboxes in steel and concrete, and you can see how vulnerable we would be to a snitch.

I can already tell that you are not the type person who would ever snitch, so I'll take time out from my story and fill you in on this mailbox thing. You see, some people don't understand the deadly serious nature of the business of knocking down mailboxes. To be recognized as an artist, you must smash not only the box, but the entire apparatus: box, post, milk can, and whatever else. It's okay to leave the pieces, but they must be SMASHED! Understand?

Now some people are dead set against artists, so they will get a steel mailbox post, put it in a ten-gallon milk can, and then fill the can with concrete. Then they concrete this whole abomination into the ground. They think this is a game or something, so they try and make things hard for you.

Here is what you do. Get a flatbed logging truck, two-ton or better (in my day most parents had one sitting around somewhere). Then you need a log chain; twenty feet ought to do it. Now you locate one of these souped-up, concrete-reinforced mailboxes, and wait for the full moon. Tie one end of the chain to the back of that old flatbed and you are ready to go. Note: You'll need a driver up front and three or four witnesses squatted down on the flatbed.

Now you're ready. The recommended speed is forty miles per hour. If the truck won't go that fast, just do the best you can. Just before you come even with the mailbox, fling that chain. Be sure and trail your target, because you're going about forty miles an hour. It's kinda like trying to rope a calf that's running backward, if you know what I mean.

Everything from this point on is fully automatic and requires absolutely no human intervention. First, the chain will wrap itself around the post of the mailbox. Next, the momentum of the truck will remove the slack from the chain. At this point the chain becomes momentarily bonded to the post. Now you will hear several sounds simultaneously. You will hear a clang, a twang, and, if the mailbox owner has done his work well, a short hum. This is because for a very short period of time you have placed EXTREME TENSION on your log chain.

The rest is sheer poetry. The log chain immediately goes limp and starts bouncing crazily around and sometimes will even jump up on the truck and knock somebody out, but that's why you brought three or four. Odds are, some will survive. The big deal now is to watch the mailbox and all its attendant paraphernalia, because it takes on a life of its own. It jumps straight up out of the ground, becomes airborne, and flies high overhead, tumbling randomly, and sometimes comes between you and the moon. If it comes down in the road, it will bounce wonderfully and break all into little pieces. A scientist would need six weeks to figure out what it originally was. It is simply beautiful.

A word of caution: There are some skills and a few details I failed to mention. Best you leave this kind of work to the professionals. If you are an amateur and try this, the chances are excellent you'll mess yourself up pretty bad. Or worse yet, you'll run over your own disaster and mess up your dad's truck.

I can't tell you about the dynamite and other stuff, because in my day, these things were classified as trade secrets, and may still be, for all I know. Besides, times have changed, and people don't fish with dynamite much any more, and that's good. But I'll tell you this: If we had stumbled across an atomic bomb, we would have headed straight for White River and blown the hell out of it. As it was, we had to make do with dynamite; it was all we had.

So you can readily see we were vulnerable to snitches. One good snitch in the right position could have done us all in. We also collectively suffered from another disability: as a general rule we wouldn't lie about anything. That doesn't mean we were defenseless. For instance, I could play brain-dead. I found this was easy, and I could do it almost perfectly without practice. I have received compliments from people I didn't even know about this talent. Members of my family tell me they think it is a natural God-given gift. Either that, or I inherited it. Sometimes I think they're trying to tell me something.

Anyway, it finally happened. My friend Dean and I discovered the existence of a snitch. We discovered this by accident, and I will tell you about that so you can see for yourself how innocent little things like knock-down-drag-out school yard fights can blow themselves up into something big if not properly managed.

It all started one afternoon during the last recess. This recess was forty-five minutes long and lasted until it was time for us to board the bus home. Now, when it comes to fights, the most important thing is to establish who started it. I know you are anxious, so I'll tell you right out: Dean started it. We came out of the school building and walked out beside a big stack of cinder blocks. On impulse, Dean grabbed my cap and threw it on top of the cinder blocks. I didn't provoke him into doing this, or if I did you can't prove it, so I think we have clearly established who started the fight. I bided my time, and soon Dean pulled his new harmonica out of his pocket and started blowing on it. I snatched it from him and threw it on top of the cinder blocks. Tit for tat you know. He couldn't play the damned thing anyway.

These things have a natural way of escalating, but in all fairness to Dean, he offered a negotiated settlement: He said if I'd get his harmonica down, he would get my cap, and all would be even. I refused. There was a reason. His harmonica had fallen into the cinder blocks, and this meant I would have to move all the blocks, then restack them. Meanwhile, there sat my hat in plain sight and easy reach.

Dean's position was that if I wouldn't negotiate, then we must fight. I agreed. I thought this was going to be easy, but it wasn't.

I thought because Dean's parents were rich and had indoor plumbing, and Dean didn't have to work as hard as I did, I should be able to whip him easy. This kind of thinking can get you skinned up pretty bad.

So we went at it. Now we couldn't really hurt each other too bad with our fists, because we were too tough and quick for that. It would help you understand if you knew that one of our favorite pastimes was for one boy to lie down flat, and the rest of the class would take turns jumping up and down on his stomach. This is what you do when you can't get a good rock fight started. But as time went by, the flint rocks and gravel began to take their toll. Blood began to flow, and socks started turning red. Clothing slowly disintegrated and knees and elbows became raw from rolling around in those flint rocks. We lost track of time.

Finally we paused for breath and realized we had overdone it. The school was deathly silent. The teachers' cars were all gone. And there sat our school bus, the engine off, the kids all jammed on our side of the bus so they could see better. And there was the bus driver, smiling, smoking a cigarette, with his feet up on the dash. God knows how long they had been sitting there. We had fought through our forty-five-minute recess and at least fifteen minutes more. This could truly be called the "Long Round."

We got on the bus, sat down together and started planning our next escapade. We were careless of the blood, because the bus driver had nine kids at home, and maybe some more that we didn't know about, and was used to blood. We didn't fear punishment, because there were no snitches on our bus. How wrong can you get?

The next day we got off the bus and walked into school as we normally did. But no sooner had we sat down than Mr. Brewer, the superintendent, walked in. He was so mad he wasn't even sniffing, and he crooked his index finger at us as if to say, "You two better come with me before I lose patience and kill you both." (I didn't learn this was an act until I became a parent.)

We went to his office, and he told me to wait outside. He took Dean inside, and I said to myself, "Maybe he already knows who started it." Soon I heard this noise, WHACK, WHACK, WHACK! I counted. Nine of them. In a minute Dean came out, smiling and rubbing his behind. He looked at me and said, "You're next; I'll wait here."

Mr. Brewer said nothing to me; he just went to work with his paddle. I guess he wasn't interested in who started the fight. WHACK, WHACK, WHACK! I counted, because I was always big on fairness. There were nine of them, so I was content.

Dean and I talked about this on the way back to class; an hour of fighting, and only nine whacks! What a deal! But we couldn't be sure; maybe they charged by the minute? We dropped that subject right away, because it involved arithmetic.

What really bothered us was the issue of the snitch. And the snitch was on our bus. We couldn't ignore this hard fact. We and all our friends were in mortal danger. Why, if left unattended, this matter could destroy our whole way of life. It was up to us to expose this nosy blabbermouth, and we felt we were up to the task. Besides, it was in the public interest; we were sure of that. We promised each other we would go home and "think on it."

Now, I know what you are thinking: maybe there wasn't a snitch after all. You are thinking, just maybe, if you see two young boys skinned and bruised from head to toe, you could figure on your own what happened without the aid of a snitch. But you're thinking too fast and getting way ahead of yourself, so just hold on while I clear this up for you.

You see, we didn't come home from school and watch TV and do homework; we did other things. Let's just suppose you were my brother, and you went to school with me: Chances are, one day your would come home and your dad would say something like this,

"Son, you know that young bull we dehorned night before last?"

"Yeah."

"Well, the flies are getting to him, and we're gonna catch him and put some more gop on them horn holes. Go get that rope that's hanging in the old henhouse, and wait for me out by the cow pen. And stay away from that bull 'til I get there."

"Okay."

You get the rope and go to the cow-pen to wait, but you're impatient; the "Suppertime Frolic" will be on the old battery radio in thirty minutes. Besides, the bull looks sick, with his head down and his eyes half-closed. And he's standing real close. So you cast your loop. Now as soon as you see you've got him, you lunge for a walnut tree, because you know with a one-half wrap you can hold a freight train, and if the bull charges, you can climb the tree. But suppose you don't quite make it.

When you don't quite make it, bad things happen. First the bull jerks you into the tree with tremendous force, and the bark and skin get all mixed up. Next, he drags you around the pasture polishing flint rocks with your exterior. You can't let go, because if you dad sees that bull running loose in the pasture with a rope around his neck, he'll kill you dead. The only thing to do is hang on until you can snag a tree with a half-wrap.

Now I know you are skeptical and want to know, did things like that really happen to me and my brothers? The answer is simple. Yes. Countless times. And to my sisters too; we were all stupid.

One last thing: Don't get the wrong idea and picture in your mind this little school filled with bandaged-up children. We didn't wear bandages. There is a reason for this: Maggots will get under a bandage, then come crawling out at the most unexpected times. This is embarrassing.

My point is simple: The only way you could tell if we had been fighting was to have seen us fighting. Only those riding our bus saw us, and someone snitched. And our job was to expose the snitch. This was our duty.

Within three days we had hatched a plan. This plan was detailed and comprehensive. It embodied mathematics, logic, law and time-proven methods of problem solving. It was exquisite, and I am proud of it even today. Too bad it didn't work out.

Problem number one: Whatever we did must be lawful, because we were going to intentionally expose ourselves to the snitch, who would, by snitching on us, expose himself to the world. There was a complication: Whatever we did must in fact appear to be unlawful, because snitches normally don't traffic in lawful affairs.

Problem number two: There were too many kids on the bus; we must find some way to systematically reduce the number of suspects before it became obvious we were setting traps.

To our credit, we decided to segment our plan. We would first reduce the number of suspects by capitalizing on our recent record of animosity toward each other. Fights are like earthquakes, you know; aftershocks are expected. Our execution was flawless; here's how it went.

I obtained a large, important-looking book that could, if necessary, clearly and absolutely be identified as NOT belonging to the school. I gave this book to Dean. We sat quietly on the school bus until approximately one-half the students had been picked up. Then we staged a modest scuffle to get everyone's attention, whereupon I grabbed the book and flung it out the window into a hay field. This spot had previously been selected, and I still remember it clearly even after fifty years. It was just after we passed the old Albert Dean place and started up the hill. Our reasoning went thusly: (a) it was perfectly permissible for me to throw my own book out the bus window (this reasoning held, but just barely), and (b) if push came to shove, we could go back and find the book.

The immediacy of the results exceeded our wildest expectations. We didn't even make it to the classroom. Here came Mr. Brewer while we were still in the hallway, and he was mad again.

He pointed his finger at me and said, "Did you throw a book out the bus window?"

"Yes, but it was my book."

"Okay, let's go."

He abruptly turned and walked out to his car, and we followed. If I remember correctly, it was a big Chrysler. I had never ridden in anything like that before. Dean and I looked at each other. This was going exactly as planned, but somehow it was much scarier than we had anticipated. We belatedly realized we were walking a tightrope, and one misstep meant disaster. Nevertheless, we were pleased that we had reduced the number of suspects by half with such ease. We were first-class detectives. With this experience under our belt, God only knew what good we would accomplish next.

We directed Mr. Brewer to the spot. Everyone dismounted, then Mr. Brewer said, "FIND THE BOOK." Mr. Brewer leaned against the front of that big Chrysler, and we began to look for the book. We looked and looked, and then we looked some more. Mr. Brewer seemed comfortable and in no hurry, so we looked some more. No luck. By and by, panic began to set in. Now panic is a subtle thing and can easily be overlooked, so I'll explain; then you'll know it next time you see it. Your knees get shaky, and there's lots of sweat under your arms. You are alternately hot and cold, and you don't think you will ever be able to eat again. It is almost impossible to breathe, and you wonder if crying would help. But worst of all, your voice cracks when you talk, and you sound like a girl.

Finally we went to Mr. Brewer and laid the whole thing out from start to finish and assured him, as God was our witness, the book was mine. He was impassive through all this, then he pointed to the field and said, "FIND THE BOOK!"

By now we were incapable of organizing any kind of systematic approach to the search other than, "You look over there, and I'll look over here," but finally we found the book.

With a sense of relief, we presented the book to Mr. Brewer. He scrutinized it carefully and then motioned us to the car. Not a word was spoken on the way back to school. But I did notice a few things: Occasionally the corner of his mouth would twitch, and he had resumed sniffing, which was a good sign.

When we parked and got out, Mr. Brewer turned to us and said, "Carl Dann snitched on you boys." He paused a moment and then added, "All you had to do was ask." He then handed me my book and went inside.

Dean and I stood there with our mouths open for a while, just looking at each other. You see, Carl Dann was a teacher who occasionally rode the bus. We didn't know if it was because his car broke down a lot or if he was just too cheap to buy gas. I guess it doesn't make any difference.

Finally Dean said, "Well, that was a waste."

"What do you mean a waste? We caught him, didn't we?"

"We didn't catch anybody, and besides, you can't catch a teacher for snitching."

"You wanna explain that?"

"Yeah. We didn't catch Carl, because Mr. Brewer snitched on him! He beat us out of it! And besides, YOU CAN'T CATCH A TEACHER FOR SNITCHING; THAT'S WHAT THEY DO FOR A LIVING! THEY GET PAID FOR SNITCHING, FOR CHRISSAKES!"

I agreed.

25

OLD FOX HUNTERS
LIKE STRONG COFFEE

By Jim Evans

In the Ozark Mountains of southern Missouri, where I grew up, fox-hunting was a popular form of recreation enjoyed by several men in our little neighborhood. Except for occasional target practice with a rifle, it was my father's only recreation. Some have said that it was his main occupation. A local preacher once said that fox hunting replaced religion for some folk.

Now this was not the type of fox hunting where men with brandy flasks and dressed in red coats, hunting caps and knee-high boots galloped horses recklessly over field and fences in pursuit of the hounds. My father and his hunting buddies would simply loose their dogs, build a campfire, and make a large pot of coffee to drink while they sat around listening to the sound of the dogs baying as they chased the fox. I have never been sure what part of the hunt they enjoyed most: the sound of dogs barking as they chased the fox over the hills or the camaraderie with their friends.

They could recognize a dog by the sound of its bark, just as most people recognize a friend or neighbor by the sound of his voice; my dad could recognize the bark of just about every foxhound from Bradleyville to Thornfield. On nights that he didn't hunt he would sometimes sit on the porch late and listen to dogs baying many miles away; often he would say something like "Ted Pellham is hunting down by Reuter tonight" or "Denver Jenkins is hunting between Bradleyville and Union Flat." I could hardly hear the dogs at that distance, much less distinguish whose dog it was. When I was about eleven or twelve years old, I occasionally accompanied my father and some of his friends on those hunts, helping to build the fire and enjoying the stories that hunters seem always to tell in such settings. I especially enjoyed it when some hunter from another part of the state came or if someone who had been on a trip was there with stories about what another part of the world was like. I never really cared just to listen to the hounds.

One of the favorite areas to meet for these hunts was a group of rocky hills around a mountaintop near Brownbranch, known by the locals as Dick Bald, now known as Bugle Mountain by the current residents. That location provided a spectacular view of the surrounding hills covered with several species of trees, such as white oak, hickory, cedar and yellowwood. The small valleys (called "hollers") were lined with species such as willow and sycamore trees. Sprinkled over the mountainsides were thousands of white dogwoods that, when in bloom, added to the unforgettable beauty of the hills. Of course, because I had never been anywhere else I didn't appreciate the beauty of the hills at that time.

The high altitude of the location, relative to the surrounding hills, provided almost perfect acoustics to hear the dogs barking over miles of mountainous terrain; this alone made it a desirable location to hear a fox chase. Another convenient feature of that location was that it was very close to Highway 76. Although it was still just a gravel road, it was passable year-round. That made it convenient for many of Dad's hunting buddies from as far away as Forsyth, or sometimes farther, to meet up with him. Dad usually walked his dogs there from our place at McClurg; he felt dogs wouldn't hunt well if they rode in a car or truck just prior to the hunt.

Two sisters named Elnora and Birdle Mannon and their elderly widowed mother lived nearby. When Dad and his friends were hunting in that area he would always stop by their house to inform them they would be hunting that night. He did this so they would know the identity of the hunters and not be concerned if they saw a campfire or heard laughter during the night. One of the Mannon sisters usually wrote a news article for the local county paper, and the sisters would often go to the campsite and visit a while to gather any news they could. This was before telephones were available in the area, and the sisters always seemed happy to see and talk with someone who might have news that was worthy of printing.

During these outings I was often assigned the chore of finding water and making coffee in a three-gallon coffeepot they used. No reliable water supply ran near their favorite campsite; therefore, it was often necessary to walk to the bottom of the mountain to find a stream with water suitable for making coffee. I soon tired of that chore.

Hoping to discourage them from assigning this unpleasant task to me, I began to make the coffee progressively stronger each time I made a new pot. Although I noticed they drank it much slower, they did not complain; I sensed that they thought it was unmanly to complain about strong coffee. They continued having me fetch water and make coffee.

One night my dad had invited a couple of his hunting buddies from the Forsyth area to hunt with us; joining us were Emmett Adams and Doc Egbert from Forsyth and Jim Owens from Branson. They arrived with three pickup trucks filled with foxhounds, more than thirty in all, of all sizes and colors. Mr. Owens operated a float-fishing business on the White River and had furnished the pickups for this hunting trip; "Jim Owens Float Fishing" was painted in bold letters on their sides.

Normally, Dad would turn only one or two dogs loose at the beginning of the hunt; these were dogs that he had trained especially to search out and force a fox to start running. He called them his jump dogs. When he heard them start the fox running, he turned the other dogs loose to enter the chase. He said if too many dogs were turned loose too soon, they usually would start several different fox chases at once. He found that annoying.

Mr. Owens had an entirely different idea about how to start a fox hunt: As soon as they parked, he turned loose all thirty of their dogs plus all my dad's. This made nearly three dozen dogs running in every direction, all barking at something, mostly one another. A couple of dogfights quickly started, adding to the noise and confusion.

Soon the dogs had started four separate fox chases in different directions; because of so many dogs baying, it was impossible to determine which dogs were running and where. I knew Dad didn't approve of hunting in that style; however, because these were old and dear friends of his, he didn't say anything. He just smiled and sat listening to the roar of dogs from every direction. Even when his most prized foxhound treed a raccoon, he said nothing. I could tell it was a major disappointment for him; he believed that if a hound started treeing it could never be a good foxhound again.

By this time most of the hunters had begun asking if coffee was ready; I had already built a fire and had the water ready for coffee when we discovered no one had brought coffee. Mr. Owens asked his driver to find a store that was still open and get some. Just as the driver was starting the pickup, Mr. Owens called out, "Be sure you get Mr. Judge brand coffee!" He laughed and added, "That Sunshine brand these guys over here drink has no kick."

After a while the driver returned with two large cans, saying he had found a store owner at Bradleyville willing to open, even at that late hour. Mr. Owens handed one can to me and said, "Kid, make us some real coffee, not the weak stuff these sissies are used to." I poured the entire can into the pot and placed it over the fire; as it began to boil, it looked more like transmission fluid than coffee.

I then lay in the shadows pretending to be asleep but really watching to see if they would drink it. They drank it very slowly, attempting not to grimace as they swallowed the bitter-tasting beverage without one complaint. While most of the hunters only took one cup, Mr. Owens drank several and loudly praised me for making such great coffee, saying, "Now this is a real man's coffee." I couldn't tell if he really did like it or if he was just goading the others because they weren't drinking much.

That was the last time I was asked to make coffee for the hunters. Every time we went out after that, Dad and his friends always seemed eager to make their own coffee.

26

BRADLEYVILLE TODAY

BY JAMES LEON COMBS

Fifty years have passed since I graduated from Bradleyville High School, sixty since the days when most of these stories took place. I have returned to my hometown after an absence of almost forty years. The basic nature of my people here has not changed; they are still independent, kind, generous and good neighbors.

While the people haven't changed much in thoughts and attitudes, their way of life bears little resemblance to that of their grandparents. New four-wheel-drive pickups have replaced Model A Fords and wagons pulled by teams of workhorses. Communication around Bradleyville in the forties was by couriers; if you needed a doctor, you walked or rode a horse or drove an old car or truck over dirt and gravel roads. There were no phones. Now, just as in the big cities, Bradleyville residents have high-speed phone lines, worldwide Internet connections, and satellite television with live coverage from around the earth and outer space. Using overnight delivery services, you can send things from the depths of these hills to anywhere in the country in twenty-four hours. Indoor plumbing replaced the outhouses, and electrical appliances crowded out washboards and wood cook stoves.

Paradoxically, while Bradleyville people may live miles apart, they are closer to their neighbors than those jammed atop one another in big cities. Here, everyone knows when you are ill, when visitors spend the night with you and just about everything else about you. They know because they care, because they want to help, to make your life more livable. Yesterday my wife asked me to take a loaf of fresh-baked bread to our neighbors, the Rev. Vernon and Barbara June Fuller. Dot called to let them know I was on my way. I drove the half-mile and pulled into their driveway only to see Vernon waiting with a plastic bag in his hands. He took the loaf of bread, thanked me and handed me the bag with three dozen fresh eggs from his flock of chickens. Vernon also has standing privileges to catch catfish from the small lake in front of our house.

There's a saying, "You can't go home again." I don't agree. I understand the thrust of the statement, however, and know that the many changes that take place over four decades of our fast-paced society make returning to family and old friends challenging. First, it's a little like flipping a switch and watching yourself and friends go from seventeen to Medicare recipients overnight. Girls with wispy blonde hair and slender lithe bodies are now grandmothers. Young guys with flexible, wiry bodies are now gray headed, paunchy, and walk carefully, hampered by muscle stiffness and arthritis.

When I was a boy, kids around Bradleyville had little contact with young people from other parts of the county. Therefore, our dress, speech, taste in music, and other things that interested young people were not in sync with more stylish city kids. It's different today because of mass communications. Bradleyville's young people dress like, talk like and listen to the same music as kids across the country. True, their world is still limited compared to those in large metropolitan areas with access to large public schools, expensive private schools, major league sports, art museums and other cultural advantages. But Bradleyville kids still swim in Beaver Creek, coon hunt the Ozarks hills and enjoy float trips and picnics. They call everyone for miles around by their first name, including the county sheriff and circuit judges.

Expectations may differ from the son or daughter of a big city doctor to a child of a working family in Bradleyville. Professional urban families likely program their children from kindergarten not only to go to college but to be accepted by one of the eastern elite universities – Harvard, Yale, Brown and other bastions of the rich and famous. Bradleyville kids' parents may or may not encourage them to finish high school and go to college. Certainly, they would not even think of sending them to one of the eastern elites; rather, graduating from a good technical or vocational school might be considered a great achievement. Success after graduation may be measured by how much per hour one earns or the amount of good he or she does for the community.

Bradleyville has its shortcomings, such as no movie theater or shopping mall, but in this day of war and terrorism, there is a certain peacefulness and comfort as you stroll through the woods or down a country lane. Stars shine brighter in the Ozarks sky. Stunning sunrises highlight valleys filled with snow-white fog, snaking its way between green hills of foliage. Farmers who have lived their lives in these hills still pause to marvel at blazing sunsets splashing the horizon, and visitors try vainly to capture nature's best with digital cameras.

Most Bradleyville people have a strong faith in their religion. They go to church two or three times a week, believing completely. Children meet their school friends in Sunday school and sing together in the choir. Fathers often defy the Supreme Court, offering up a prayer at graduation and other school events; no one complains.

But there is another side to our town that may show up at the Pizza Parlor on Saturday night. A small country-western band usually entertains while some locals relax to a few drinks and round dancing. The fights sometimes start around midnight and spill out onto the gravel parking lot. Strong young men who spend their lives doing honest manual labor will battle over some real or imagined insult, even though they may have known each other since the first grade. When Monday morning rolls around, the combatants are likely to be working side by side.

A county sheriff's deputy who receives the call about a fight in Bradleyville is likely to take his time getting there, having learned that breaking up a fight at the Pizza Parlor can be hazardous.

Bradleyville is a microcosm of our country with most of the best and a little of the worst. It is a place you can go home to – I know, I did. Bradleyville is my hometown.

MEET THE AUTHOR

James Leon Combs was born in Forsyth and raised in Bradleyville, Missouri. As a youth, he worked at various jobs, ranging from helping his parents run their general store to driving trucks in wheat and pea harvests in Oregon and Washington.

He attended Southwest Missouri State College in Springfield his freshman year, then served three years in the U. S. Marine Corps. Combs then entered the University of Missouri in Columbia, earning a bachelor of journalism degree in 1960. He worked for Jostens yearbook division for 25 years, retiring in 1985 after leading the company in sales for 15 consecutive years. Combs owned various businesses in the St. Louis area until he and his wife, Dorothy, retired to their new home on Bugle Mountain in Bradleyville, where they own the 3,000-acre Beaver Creek Elk & Cattle Ranch.

HOW TO ORDER MORE COPIES OF

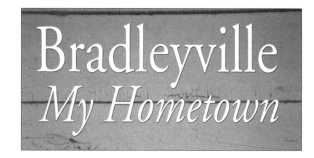

or
Bradleyville Basketball
The Hicks from the Sticks

Major bookstores
Amazon.com
Beaver Creek Publishing, L. L. C.
P.O. Box 2000
Bradleyville, Missouri 65614
888-225-9400
JLCombs13@aol.com
www.bradleyvillehometown.com
www.bradleyvillebasketball.com